The Bhagavad Gita is unquestionably the m
among our holy books. The deepest reason wh
aspiring hearts is that Krishna's divine song is, i
convincing gospel ever preached by a Messia
valuable aid for understanding the supreme en
of wisdom (*jnana*), love (*bhakti*) and action (*karma*). By rendering the Sanskrit divine song into English blank verse, Dilip Kumar Roy has done a literary miracle which only he could perform. His interpretation of the message of the Gita is conspicuous by its freshness, simplicity and relevance to modern life.

Dilip Kumar Roy, a product of Calcutta and Cambridge Universities, received his well-rounded musical training in Germany and Italy before returning to India. At the age of 31 he was initiated into spiritualism by Sri Aurobindo. He has authored some sixty books in English and Bengali.

"Not only sweet but also scintillating."

— Deccan Herald

"Marks the peak of author's ability to render Sanskrit original without robbing it of its dignity and compactness."

— Triveni

The Bhagavad Gita

A REVELATION

Dilip Kumar Roy

HIND POCKET BOOKS

THE BHAGAVAD GITA

2nd edition 1993
ISBN 81-216-0284-X

Published by
Hind Pocket Books (P) Ltd.
Editorial office: C-36, Connaught Place
New Delhi-110001
H.O.: G.T. Road, Shahdara, Delhi-110032

Typeset at Quick Photocomposers
New Delhi-110 055

Printed at Thomson Press, Faridabad (Haryana)

PRINTED IN INDIA

CONTENTS

FOREWORD

I FEEL happy to be asked by Dilip Kumar Roy, *sura-sudhākar*, to write a Foreword to his translation of the Bhagavad Gita. After reading the typescript I have not a shred of doubt in mind that his rendering is going to enhance his reputation as a translator. The work, in blank verse, does retain the dignity and grandeur of this supreme metre in English poetry.

In the opening chapter, Dhṛtarāṣṭra asks Saṁjaya, his friend and charioteer, to relate to him from day to day all that transpires on the battlefield of Kurukṣetra — Dharma*kṣetra*, the arena of dharma. The question asks itself whether the world we live in is a dharma*kṣetra* as well. Do not grim struggles go on and are not momentous issues fought out amidst conditions as difficult as they are perplexing and mysterious ? We are not told why we are here on this planet and for how long. History teaches us that the span of human life is brief and, ordinarily, when we grapple with life, we find that the problems which beset us are formidable enough in all conscience. We rely on our Reason to start with, but gradually come to discover, alas, that it fails us in the end! Then we tell ourselves : "Why bother, since we come, stay and depart at His will ? Is not the world, He chooses to seek birth in time and again, His dear playground where He comes to play at hide and seek with us ?" The rationalist who idolises reason scoffs at such puerile illusions of blind faith but when mental reason eventually lets him down he has, perforce, to do some rethinking. How does he actually proceed then ? He may look round for a guide to lead him home, but who can be an infallible guide in this our distracted world ? So, the Lord answers Arjuna : "When you fail to find the clue to light in life's blinding darkness, turn to me and I will direct you along the path you must tread to attain the Goal of lasting Bliss and Harmony. As for the man in the street," He goes on to add, "he should approach an illuminate, bow down at his feet, ask him questions about the Way and, lastly, serve him as best he can." (The Gita, 4.34)

So long, however, as our ego holds the sway and reason serves as the minister, we are not only led astray but must end in the blind alley of unutterable bewilderment. That is why, when Arjuna was in the grip of despair he had to appeal to Kṛṣṇa (The Gita, 2.7):

Afflicted with the weakness of self-pity,
With my mind in a turmoil, I see no way out.
So, in this blind gloom flash thy lead of light
To me, thy disciple : I seek refuge in thee.

The Gita enjoins a life of action. One must bear in mind that this active life should be led in such a way that it will not tie him down to the consequences his *karma* entails. But how to live such a life? The answer is : with the unerring light of knowledge. More specifically, one must offer whatever one does—all *karma*—to Him, our master, for only then can one obviate the danger of getting bound by the chains of one's *karma*.

"But why must we offer our *karma* to Him ?" We enquire. The answer is : "Because He loves us and so we too must respond to Him with our love." But how do we know that He loves us ?" we ask. The answer again is: "Because He never deserts us, our weaknesses and limitations notwithstanding. Besides, He, being our Maker cannot help but dwell in us even as the artist dwells in what he creates." In other words, presiding in us, He can never forsake us for a moment, and this being so, is it not incumbent on us to aspire to love and serve Him and offer Him all we do, have and are ? This is the keynote of what the Gita calls *niṣkāma karma*, dispassionate action, illumined by knowledge and inspired by love.

Such an inspired and illumined action, however, cannot be achieved till we grow to realise Him by dint of our love for and knowledge of Him as our hearts' one Lord and Beloved. How can such a divine Master of our destiny ever turn away from us because of our lapses and stumblings, declining to accept in Grace all that we lay at His feet, however humble the offering ? (The Gita, 9.26)

In his Introduction Dilip Kumar explains a few interesting points dealt with in the Gita.

First, the concept of svadharma, that is, the vocation assigned to us by the Supreme Ordainer.

Secondly, the truth about the Divine Personality of Kṛṣṇa, "The Myriad One", — In every heart is hidden the Myriad One... (*Sāvitri*, Sri Aurobindo) — a *pūrṇa-avatāra* (Complete Incarnation) who invites us to approach Him, following any path congenial to us, assuring us that He will receive us lovingly at the Journey's End, because He is as eager to meet us as we are to meet Him. In fact we need not give in to despair even if we fail to aspire for Him with single-minded devotion because He can be propitiated even with a partial dedication.

Thirdly, Dilip Kumar, like many a thinker, thrashes out the problem of how to tread the triune path of Yoga, to wit, of *jñāna*, *bhakti* and *karma*. In his commentary he has cited relevant and luminous passages from the Gita bearing on this theme albeit, as a devout *bhakta* by temperament, he answers wholeheartedly the call of *bhakti* (devotion) and the gospel of the *bhakta* (devotee).

Fourthly, he adumbrates the triple gunas elaborated by his Guru, Sri Aurobindo in his *Essays on the Gita*.

In conclusion, I should like to reiterate that Dilip Kumar's Translation and Essay should not be looked upon as a mere scholarly exegesis of one who is at home in both Sanskrit and English, but should be hailed as the spontaneous and felicitous self-expression of a *bhakta*, who is not only aware of His footsteps but also hears the call of His Flute as well.

GOURINATH SHASTRI
(Quondam Vice-Chancellor of
All-India Sanskrit University, Varanasi)

CONTEXT

KṚṢṆA chanted the Gita to Arjuna in an unbelievable context: the battlefield of Kurukṣetra. Many a modern scholar has given his learned verdict that it is highly unrealistic and so must have been an interpolation. But the context is extremely important and apposite, which is, surely, one of the reasons why the Gita has fascinated millions of saints and sages, prophets and illuminates who have acclaimed it all as a marvellous song of songs — a scriptural verdict of dharma against wickedness. And the message is conveyed in such a wonderful and simple verse to give the lead of Kṛṣṇa's light that it has not dimmed at all in the course of the millennia — an astonishing fact which bears out the believers' thesis that it is *apauruṣeya,* that is, a *Revelation* of the highest mystic Truth. And it is a lofty Truth harmonising action, knowledge and devotion (*karma, jñāna* and *bhakti*) a magic evangel or, shall we say, Kṛṣṇa's clue to Light in the dark labyrinth of life. We, His devotees, subscribe to this view accepting in toto the historicity of Kṛṣṇa and the Kuru-Pāṇḍava War which symbolised the immemorial tussle of righteousness with iniquity, truth with falsehood, justice with injustice, a tussle that began from the dawn of time and comes, intermittently to a head in crucial moments of history. So the reader of the Gita must be put abreast of the story of the *Mahābhārata,* the greatest Indian epic of wisdom and wonder, a veritable encyclopaedia of dharma and ethics, knowledge and wisdom — an inspiring drama of nobility and manliness at war with malevolence and chicanery.

The long story cannot be told in full, so the context is given here in brief.

Dhṛtarāṣṭra and Pāṇḍu were brothers. As the former was blind, Pāṇḍu, the younger brother, was coronated the King. He had two wives: Kuntī and Mādrī. Kuntī gave birth to three sons : Yudhiṣṭhira, Bhīma and Arjuna and Mādrī to two : Nakula and Sahadeva. When Pāṇḍu died Mādrī entered his funeral pyre; so Kuntī, an ideal mother and a devotee of Kṛṣṇa, took under her wing Nakula and Sahadeva also, along with her own sons.

Dhṛtarāṣṭra had a hundred sons : the eldest Duryodhana with his brother Duḥśāsana were his favourites, and were primarily responsible for the fraticidal Kurukṣetra war when Duryodhana ascended the throne.

After Pāṇḍu's sudden death Dhṛtarāṣṭra — who though a weak father, was not a bad man at heart — had divided the kingdom justly — one-half to be ruled by Yudhiṣṭhira, the other half by Duryodhana.

As the Pāṇḍavas (sons of Pāṇḍu) were highly gifted and powerful they prospered under the aegis of Yudhiṣṭhira who was a luminous protagonist of truth, virtue, love and righteousness. Duryodhana, who had, from the first, hated his cousins, now grew inordinately jealous of their increasing fame and popularity and wanted to do them to death. But as he failed everytime he resorted to a ruse.

Yudhiṣṭhira, though a saintly soul, had a congenital weakness for gambling, at dice, in which Śakuni, the brother-in-law of Dhṛtarāṣṭra and the chief monitor of Duryodhana, was an adept and a sharper, besides. So he challenged Yudhiṣṭhira, and, playing dishonestly, won game after game. Yudhiṣṭhira lost his head and went on staking his wealth, his kingdom, his brothers, himself, and last, his Queen Draupadī, with the result that the Pāṇḍavas became literally bond slaves to Duryodhana. But worse was to come.

Elated by his signal success, Duryodhana, to humiliate his cousins, ordered Duḥśāsana to hail Draupadī to the Court and disrobe her in public. Duḥśāsana, a scoundrel to his finger-tips, dragged her by the hair and started doing the bidding of his elder brother. At this point Draupadī prayed in tears to Kṛṣṇa, who, presiding invisibly, worked a stupendous miracle : Draupadī's sari became endless — one sari succeeded another — so she could not be deprived of her clothes. An ugly scene — almost unbelievable in its shameless and malignant cruelty — but the courtiers were all astounded by the miracle and broke into a hallelujah!

The blind king Dhṛtarāṣṭra, who had been silent all along, now intervened, deeply moved by Draupadī's prayer and insisted that the Pāṇḍavas be set at liberty and their kingdom restored to them at once.

But the blind king was a weak paterfamilias especially vis-a-vis Duryodhana who got round him again to permit another game of dice. So Śakuni challenged Yudhiṣṭhira once more and the dice-gamble was resumed. But this time the stake was different; it was stipulated that the losers would have to forefeit their kingdom and live exiled for twelve long years in the forest after which they must live for another year in some place, incognito, where they could not be traced. If they were discovered they would have to go into exile again for twelve years.

This game, too, Yudhiṣṭhira lost and so had to retire deep into the forest with his brothers and Queen Draupadī. During this period, however, the Pāṇḍavas grew in spiritual stature and Arjuna, blest by the gods, acquired a complete mastery in archery.

When thirteen years had slowly glided by, and Yudhiṣṭhira with his brothers and Queen Draupadī lived as honoured guests of King Virāta — now one of his most powerful and helpful allies — Kṛṣṇa visited them and offered to act as a messenger of the Pāṇḍavas whom he dearly loved, especially Arjuna. He drove in a splendid chariot to the palace of Duryodhana and asked him to redeem his promise. But Duryodhana flatly refused : "Let them fight back to possession if they hanker after any territory." Kṛṣṇa advised, argued and pleaded but, alas, in vain ! Duryodhana was adamant. So Kṛṣṇa returned to Yudhiṣṭhira and put him wise to all that had happened.

Duryodhana now made one last astute attempt to enlist Kṛṣṇa on his side. But Kṛṣṇa, who was a master of psychology, proposed: "You can have either my shock troops, the *Nārāyaṇī senā*, or you can have me alone. But I shall act only as a counsellor and take no active part in the actual fighting on the battlefield." Duryodhana, reassured that Kṛṣṇa would not fight, put his foot in the trap and acclaimed his redoubtable shock troops. In great jubilation he reported it all to his father, exulting and vaunting like a grand hero and diplomat.

On the other side, Yudhiṣṭhira hailed Kṛṣṇa — who, he knew, was God incarnate — and Kṛṣṇa accepted to be Arjuna's charioteer. Although Pāṇḍavas were blest by Kṛṣṇa, they could assemble only seven battalions against the Kauravas' eleven. An unequal fight. Only Lord Kṛṣṇa was there to tip the balance in the Pāṇḍavas' favour. They were overjoyed that he would be their friend, philosopher and guide.

The internecine battle was fought in the vast field of Kurukṣetra whither pilgrims still go repeating Kṛṣṇa's name.

The actual fighting lasted eighteen days and ended with total defeat of Duryodhana.

But to come back to the context, the dramatic scene of the Gita. Arjuna before sounding the final war-conch asked Kṛṣṇa to place his chariot between the two armies confronting one another so he might take final stock of the situation and survey Duryodhana with his henchmen in battle array. Kṛṣṇa complied, and the great dialogue of the Gita began — a drama par excellence !

Now it so happened that the blind king Dhṛtarāṣṭra was extremely eager to keep abreast of the day-to-day progress of the battle. The mighty Sage Vyāsa offered to restore his sight. But Dhṛtarāṣṭra, a coward at heart, quailed as he could not bear to see any of his sons killed. So Vyāsa conferred the twin occult powers of clairvoyance and clairaudience on Saṁjaya the blind king's minister as well as charioteer. As they sat together side by side in the royal palace Saṁjaya graphically described to his master everything that happened on the battlefield. He began his recital of the first Act of the great drama by reporting verbatim how Arjuna's chariot flashed roaring on the battlefield and in what context the Lord sang His immortal Gita or shall we say, an exhortation to the Life Divine through a marvellous synthesis of the three Yogas — of action, knowledge and devotion (*karma*, *jñāna* and *bhakti*).

In his masterly essay, *Notes on the Mahābhārata*, Sri Aurobindo wrote :

And when in the immense lapse of time it (the Yoga of the Gita) was lost Sri Kṛṣṇa again declared it to a Kṣatriya. But when the Kṣatriyas disappeared, the Brahmins remained the sole interpreters of the Bhagavad-Gita... and their thoughts therefore naturally turned to knowledge and the final end of being... They have laid stress on the goal, but they have not echoed Sri Kṛṣṇa's emphasis on the necessity of action as the one sure road to the Goal. Time, however, in its revolution is turning back on itself and there are signs that if Hinduism is to last and we are not to plunge into the vortex of scientific atheism and the breakdown of moral ideals which is engulfing Europe, it must survive as the religion of Vyāsa for which Vedānta, Sāṁkhya and Yoga combined to lay the foundations, which Sri Kṛṣṇa announced and which Vyāsa formulated.

The Gita

DHṚTARĀṢṬRA

When in Kurukṣetra's sacred battlefield
Pāṇḍu's belligerent sons and my own met,
What happened, Saṁjaya tell me in detail. (1.1)

SAṀJAYA

When Duryodhana reviewed the Pāṇḍavas'
Great army, he said to his teacher, Droṇa :
"Master, behold the mighty phalanxed hordes
Of the Pāṇḍavas led by the son of Drupada..."
Then the war-mooded chieftains of both sides
In chorus blew their terrific deafening conchs. (1.2 — 19, gist)

Arjuna asked his charioteer, Lord Kṛṣṇa :
"Draw up, my friend, our battle-car between
Their army and our own, so I may now
Survey the battle-array... Accordingly
Kṛṣṇa complied and said : "Behold, my friend !" (1.21 — 25, gist)

When Arjuna was confronted with his kin,
A deep pity invaded his heart. He said :
"O Kṛṣṇa, when I see them now, I feel
No more a desire for victory, kingdom or joys..."
And so he moaned on in dejection till
He threw away his mighty bow and quiver. (1.26 — 46, gist)

SAṀJAYA

Then Madhusūdan Kṛṣṇa, seeing Arjuna
Unmanned by melancholy, rebuked him thus : (2.1)

KṚṢṆA

Whence has swooped down on you this sudden and morbid
Depression in the hour of crisis and peril ?

Is it worthy of you, a scion of noble birth,
This disgraceful mood that never can lead to heaven ? (2.2)

Yield not to sentimental cowardice :
It behoves you not. Disclaim once and for all
This faintheartedness. Rise to the occasion ! (2.3)

ARJUNA

But how could I, O friend, wound with my arrows
Droṇa, my teacher and Bhīṣma, my grandsire,
My seniors whom I ought to adore and worship ?
'Twere better to live in the world by begging alms
Than to slay our honoured elders. Oh, if I
Did them to death, how could I ever thereafter
Enjoy this ghastly bloodstained victory ? (2.4 — 5)

Nor do I know which truly is preferable :
Their victory or ours after this dreadful carnage ?
For we would not care to live if these our people
Who challenge us were slain by us in battle. (2.6)

Afflicted with the weakness of self-pity,
With my mind in a turmoil, I see no way out.
So in this blind gloom flash thy lead of light
To me, thy disciple : I seek refuge in thee. (2.7)

For even if I win a prosperous and unrivalled
Kingdom on earth or sovereignty of the gods
I cannot see how I'll deliver my soul
From the pain of massacre desiccating the senses. (2.8)

SAṀJAYA

Appealing thus to Kṛṣṇa, Arjuna said:
"I will not fight" and bowed his head in silence. (2.9)

With the chariot placed between the armies, Kṛṣṇa
Addressed Arjuna with a smile of irony. (2.10)

KṚṢṆA

You wail for those for whom you never should grieve
And withal, speak with the accent of the wise !
But the truly wise grieve neither for the dead
Nor for the living. Never was there a time
When you or I or these chieftains and kings
Were non-existent. Nor shall ever come
A time when any of us will cease to exist. (2.11 — 12)

As the soul fares ever on through childhood, youth
And old age, when a person breathes his last,
It journeys on to assume another body :
So no true sage is ever deceived by death. (2.13)

The contact of the senses with their objects
Gives rise to cold and heat, pleasure and pain :
They come and go, nor last forever. So
Such transient things you must learn to endure. (2.14)

He who is not affected by these contacts
Of the senses with their objects and stays unmoved
By joy or pain attains to blessedness.
That which is non-existent never can
Come into being nor it can ever
Cease to be. The illuminates have all
Attested this in their experience.
Know this — the One who pervades this universe
Is indestructible, and none can ever
Succeed in changing the Immutable. (2.15 — 17)

Only the material forms, assumed by the Soul,
Which is the fathomless and eternal, come to an end.

So you must fight ever on without a qualm.
Neither he who thinks he can kill the Soul.
Nor he who thinks It is killed knows the truth :
For It can neither kill nor ever be killed.
One is never born nor dies at any time
Nor once he comes to be, ever cease to be.
Unborn, immutable, eternal, ageless,
The Soul is not slain when the body's slain.
Who knows this Soul as indestructible,
Immutable, eternal and increate
How can he slay or cause It to be slain ? (2.18 — 21)

Even as a man discards his worn-out robe
For a new one, so a worn-out body is
Left by the Soul for a new one after death.
Weapons can never cleave nor fire burn
Water drench nor wind desiccate the Soul. (2.22 — 23)

'Tis incombustible, uncleavable,
It can neither be drenched nor desiccated. Eternal,
Immutable and still, it pervades all. (2.24)

It is unmanifest, immutable,
Unthinkable and inconceivable,
So knowing this, you must grieve nevermore. (2.25)

But if you think the soul is constantly
Born to die thereafter, even then
You should not grieve to no purpose, my friend ! (2.26)

The one who is born must die even as the one
Who dies shall be reborn in due course. So
Grieve no more for the ineluctable. (2.27)

One is unmanifest at the beginning,
Manifest in the middle and becomes

Unmanifest in the end once more. So what
Is there so tragic about this law of life ? (2.28)

Some see the Soul as a strange thing, while some others
Describe It as mysterious and strange
And there are those who find It stranger still
When they hear about It. None has plumbed It yet. (2.29)

The One who dwells in all is everliving,
So, how can the Eternal ever be slain ?
Therefore, friend, you should grieve for none on earth. (2.30)

Further, having regard for what is assigned
As your duty, you must never vacillate :
For the highest call a Kṣatriya (warrior) can answer
Is to stand and fight for a cause approved by dharma. (2.31)

Thrice-blessed is that Kṣatriya
Who is called to such a war by destiny,
A war to be hailed as an open door to heaven. (2.32)

But if you refuse to acclaim such a war, enjoined
By dharma, you shall incur sin, thus declining
To respond to such a great and glorious call. (2.33)

Slain, you shall go to heaven, and if you win,
You shall enjoy the earth at your feet. So, rise,
O friend, to the occasion, vowed to fight. (2.37)

Look upon joy and pain with an equal eye
May never the thought of loss or gain affect you,
Let victory or defeat be the same to you
Thus you must, friend, fight on and, when you do,
No shadow of sin shall ever taint your life. (2.38)

In the Yoga of action nothing you undertake
Can ever be vain, nor obstacles prevail.

For even an iota of righteousness,
Friend, shall deliver you from cosmic fear. (2.40)

The intellect of one who comes to accept
This Yoga is one-pointed and steadfast.
But the intellect of one who vacillates
Is many-mooded and his mind's distraught. (2.41)

Those who have little discernment and swear by
The letter of the Vedas and assert
That naught else can avail, who are attached
To the joys of paradise and are enthralled
By lovely words which drive them ever on, —
Such seekers, swept away by the Vedas' findings
(As interpreted by them), are led astray
And so their intellect can never be vowed
To cleave unwavering to the Goal — to be
Poised in the radiant Superconsciousness. (2.42 — 44)

The Vedas only deal with the three modes:
But you, Arjuna, must learn to transcend the Vedas
And the ambit of dualities. And firmly
Poised in purity, care neither to hoard
Nor acquire, conscious always of your Self. (2.45)

As when the land is flooded, the reservoir
Is superfluous, even so to the illuminate
Brāhmin the Vedas are superfluous. (2.46)

You have the right to works — not to their fruits
Which never must motivate your action on earth,
Nor must you yield to attachment to inaction. (2.47)

Poised in the Yoga, plunge in action, disowning
All attachment, may failure or success
Be one to you — for Yoga is, in essence,
Looking on all things with an equal eye. (2.48)

Action is far inferior to the Yoga
Of intelligence. So you must seek refuge
In the intellect. They are surely to be pitied
Who hanker after the fruit of every action. (2.49)

One who is poised in his intelligence
Transcends the duality of good and evil.
So strive for Yoga : Yoga is skill in works. (2.50)

The wise who merge their intellect in Him,
Renouncing the fruit of all their actions on earth,
Are freed forever from the bondage of birth
And attain the ultimate and sorrowless state. (2.51)

When your intelligence shall have overpassed
Delusion's phantom wood you shall become
Indifferent to all you have heard and all
That is yet to be heard — vain words, words, words ! (2.52)

When your intellect which now is bewildered by
The Vedas' lore will stay still in the spirit's
Samadhi — then shall you attain to the Yoga. (2.53)

ARJUNA

What is the sign of the man who is *sthitaprajña* ?
(One who lives in the light of stable wisdom)
And how does he who is called *sthitadhī* speak ?
How does he walk, sit, speak, comport himself ? (2.54)

KṚṢṆA

When one shuns all desires that derive
From the mind and ever abides in his inmost self
He wins to the stable yogic state in life.
(He is hailed by the sages as a *sthitaprajña.*) (2.55)

One who is unperturbed by grief or pain
Nor hankers ever for joy or happiness
And has overcome attachment, fear and anger,
Wins to the status of the tranquil sage.
(*Such a saint is entitled 'sthitadhī'.*) (2.56)

Who stays immune in all things from attachment,
And, visited by evil or good fortune,
Neither, resents nor feels elated — is
One whose intelligence is poised in wisdom.
Who can recall his senses from the objects
Perceived, even as a snail recalls its limbs,
Is one whose intelligence is poised in wisdom. (2.57 — 58)

Desires of the senses are subdued by one
Who abstains from all sensual enjoyments
But the taste for such thrills does still survive, only
When the Lord is seen this taste departs forever. (2.59)

The cravings of the senses are so strong
That even the conscientious, lessoned in self-control,
Succumb in life sometimes to their assaults. (2.60)

He who has controlled his senses should stay firm
In Yoga, engrossed in me; the intellect
Of one who has mastered his senses remains stable. (2.61)

When a man dwells on the objects of sense he gets
Attached to them. From attachment springs desire,
Thwarted desire gives rise to anger which
Entails bewilderment and then the loss
Of memory abrogating intelligence
Which must lead in the end to his downfall. (2.62 — 63)

But a disciplined man even when he parleys
With the objects of sense — with his senses under control

And thus free from attachment and illusion —
Attains in the end to serenity of spirit. (2.64)

And in the spirit's serenity he attains
The terminus of sorrow ; the intellect
Of such a man finds soon the poise of peace. (2.65)

Who are not yogis have no wisdom, and those
Who are not wise are not God-mooded, and the ones
Who are not God-mooded have no peace on earth
And how can they who are peaceless ever be happy ? (2.66)

When the mind goes on chasing the roving senses,
It carries away the intellect — even as
The wind carries away a boat on the waters. (2.67)

And so he who has withdrawn his senses from
Their objects has attained a stable wisdom. (2.68)

What is night to the common man is welcomed as
Day by the wakeful and what is termed day
By the common man to the illuminate looms as night. (2.69)

Even as when the waves rush into the vast
Ocean it remains tranquil, so the great
Souls stay ever unperturbed when the senses' billows
Assail them; only these attain to peace
Not those who crave for the pleasures of the senses. (2.70)

The one who disowns all desires and fares
In life transcending finally the last traces
Of craving, pride or attachment wins to peace. (2.71)

This is the *Brāhmī sthiti*, poise divine,
Which, once attained, delivers you forever
From all illusion and wins you the bliss

Of Mergence in the supernal consciousness
(Entitled *brahma nirvāṇa* by the sages). (2.72)

ARJUNA

If thou thinkest, Lord, that the path of understanding
Is superior to that of works, why then
Must thou appoint me to this dreadful mission ?
Thou dost bewilder my intelligence
With dictums that sound contradictory.
So, tell me, once for all, I pray, what is
The course that will lead me to my soul's weal. (3.1 — 2)

KṚṢṆA

I have said already that in this world there are
Two disciplines : One is the Yoga of knowledge
Practised by contemplatives, the other — the Yoga
Of works which votaries of action favour. (3.3)

By mere abstention from work none can hope
To achieve in life the peace of actionlessness,
Nor by mere renunciation can one ever
Attain to the bliss of ultimate perfection.
For no one can repudiate for a moment
The yoke of action — he being helplessly
Driven to act by the triple modes of Nature. (3.4 — 5)

He is insincere and harbours deep delusion
Who only abstains from the sensual revels
But dwells on them with mental delectation. (3.6)

He who controls his senses by the mind
Nor is attached to his action when he employs
His senses to do his duty achieves distinction.
Stay active all the time, for action is
To be preferred to indolence : even your body

Shall perish if you give in to inaction.
An action done not as a sacrifice
Forges but chains that bind the doer on earth.
So may whatever you do be an act of worship. (3.7 — 8)

Thus Prajapati (the Demi-urge) of old
Created men and enjoined them to do
All duty as a sacrifice. He said :
" Only the work which is done in this spirit
Can grant you the miracle boons you crave on earth.
(Like *Kāmadhenu*, the legendary cow,
The heavenly wish-fulfiller of men on earth.)
With sacrifice you hail the gods in heaven
And they too, in return, propitiated,
Come to bless you which is the consummation
Of all you desire (the circuit thus completed)
And as the gods, pleased by your sacrifice,
Give you boons to delight you, be forewarned :
They are but thieves who, having received their gifts,
Offer them nothing in their turn. Who eat
What, after the offering, the gods leave over,
Are delivered from sin. But those who cook their food
Only for themselves eat not food but sin. (3.10 — 13)

But the man who rejoices in his self alone
And feels complete fulfilment in his Self,
For him remains no work to be done on earth.
He has nothing to gain through action nor through actions
Left undone : to none he appeals for help :
Having no personal need for an asylum. (3.17 — 18)

So do your duty you must, dispassionately,
The ones who so act shall attain salvation. (3.19)

Janaka and others won to the soul's fulfilment
Through action. Besides, to make the world go round,
It is incumbent on you to welcome action. (3.20)

The example set by the elect is followed
By the rest : What great men initiate is hailed
As the ideal by the commonalty. (3.21)

In the three worlds, friend, I am not duty-bound
To do works nor have anything to gain
That I need to gain — and yet I am always active. (3.22)

If I did not plunge into action sleeplessly
People would emulate me in every way,
And the world would fall in ruin and I would be
Responsible for its deep disintegration. (3.23 — 24)

The ignorant act as puppets of attachment :
The wise, delivered forever from all attachments,
Act in life only to sustain the world. (3.25)

Let the illuminates not unsettle the minds
Of the ignorant who are attached to action
They should act always in the spirit of Yoga
And encourage the common man to be ever active. (3.26)

'Tis Nature (*Prakṛti*) which does all actions,
But the fool egoist thinks *he* is the doer. (3.27)

But one who knows, friend, the true principles
And divisions of the triple modes and works
And has seen that it is the modes which act
On the modes — such a man steers clear of all attachment. (3.28)

Let not the illuminates advise the unwise.
Who are Nature's puppets, to abstain from action. (3.29)

Led by the discriminative intelligence
Fight cheerfully on, offering your works to me,
Expecting no reward or recognition. (3.30)

Who full of faith and free from cavil follow
This teaching of mine steadfastly shall be
Released in due course from the bondage of works.
But those who carp at my teaching and refuse
To accept my lead of light know them to be
Blind to all wisdom, senseless and waylost. (3.31 — 32)

Everyone acts impelled by his own nature :
Even the illuminate is no exception.
How then can inhibition avail in life ? (3.33)

For either aversion or attachment must
Follow whenever the senses turn to things
Of the world, so never come under their sway. (3.34)

'Tis wiser to follow a line of evolution
Consonant with one's nature even when
'Tis imperfect than to tread to perfection a path
Alien to one's native temperament.
Even if following your own duty you die,
Cleave to it : for to follow another's duty
Shall lead your soul into a serious peril. (3.35)

ARJUNA

But what is it that compels man as it were
To perpetrate what he knows in his heart as sin ? (3.36)

KṚṢṆA

They are lust and anger, derived from the mode
Of *rajas* — they are unappeasable
And deadly — mark them as your eternal foes. (3.37)

As fire is enveloped by smoke, a mirror by dust,
An embryo by the womb — even so knowledge

Of the wise is covered by the flames of lust
Which never can be sated by any fuel. (3.38 — 39)

The senses, mind and intellect of a man
Are the time-old haunts of this relentless lust
Which veils his knowledge to delude his soul.
Therefore you ought to control first your senses
And do to death this fiendish foe which stands
In the way of wisdom and discrimination. (3.40 — 41)

The senses are commendable; the mind
Is greater than the senses; greater still
Is intelligence and the greatest of all is He.
Thus knowing Him, the Divine, who is beyond
The intelligence — you must subdue your mind,
And by your soul's own light slay once for all
This redoubtable and elusive enemy — lust. (3.42 — 43)

This imperishable Yoga I had first explained
To Vivasvān, the Sungod, who revealed it
To Manu who told it to Ikṣvāku, and so
It came down the dynasty of royal sages
Till it was lost through the long lapse of time.
This great old gospel I have now revived
To enlighten you, my friend and devotee ! (4.1 — 3)

ARJUNA

But as Vivasvān was born before thy advent,
How couldst thou have imparted it to him ? (4.4)

KṚṢṆA

Many a time, friend, were you born on earth;
I know it all but you have yet to know. (4.5)

Though in my self-existence I'm the unborn
And sempiternal Lord of all that is,
Yet standing on my own Nature I take birth
By my creative urge known as self-*māyā*. (4.6)

Whenever (dharma) righteousness declines
And there is an uprise of iniquity,
I loose myself forth into birth in the world. (4.7)

For the protection of the holy men,
The chastisement of the wicked and the enthroning
Of dharma I am born from age to age. (4.8)

My birth and action are divine, he who
Has realised this truly is not born
Ever again, for he comes home to me. (4.9)

Conquering attachment, fear and wrath, and rapt
In me and seeking refuge in me alone,
Many an illuminate has attained my status
Purged by the fire of this great mystic knowledge. (4.10)

Men approach me constantly in various ways
And I answer to each in the way he wants to meet me;
He cannot help but follow the path I tread. (4.11)

Most men desire the fruition of their works
By worshipping the gods in this our world.
Such material boons are quickly won. (4.12)

I classed men into four castes and assigned
Different functions to them in accordance
With their different temperaments and karma. But
Though I'm their author, you must bear in mind
I am myself beyond all change or action. (4.13)

No works contaminate me. Nor do I hanker
After their fruits. He who realises this
Can nevermore be bound by works on earth. (4.14)

Of old, your forbears, pining for salvation,
Performed the works inspired by this knowledge :
Even so you must follow their example. (4.15)

Even the wise are often at a loss
To know what is right action and what is wrong.
So I'll impart to you the knowledge which
Shall deliver you from all perils and misconceptions. (4.16)

One has to understand what action is,
What is wrong action and what is inaction.
'Tis difficult to know the way of works. (4.17)

He who sees truly action in inaction
And inaction in action, is the illuminate,
For he takes it all in comprehensively. (4.18)

The man whose initiatives and undertakings
Are delivered from the last taint of desire,
Whose works are burnt up by the fire of knowledge
Is to be entitled an illuminate. (4.19)

Such a man has abandoned all attachment
To the fruits of his works, he's always satisfied.
He has no need to depend on anyone
And does nothing even when engaged in action.
(For it is Nature which works in and through him.) (4.20)

Who has no desires and whose heart and self
Are under control and who performs all works
With his body alone — such a man commits no wrong. (4.21)

Who is content with whatever accrues to him,
Who's beyond the dualities of pleasure and pain,
Who is not jealous of anyone and remains
Calm, unaffected by failure or success,
Such a man is not bound even when he acts. (4.22)

One who is liberated, free from all
Attachments and whose mind is founded in
Self-knowledge, when such an illuminate
Does works as a sacrifice they are all dissolved,
(His actions forge no chain of consequences). (4.23)

For him the act of offering is God,
God is the oblation and He offers the food,
Haviḥ, to the fire of God, in whom he yearns
To merge in samadhi through his God-rapt action. (4.24)

Who eat the sacred food that is first offered
As a sacrifice attain the eternal God.
Even this world is not for him who offers
No sacrifice in life — so how can he
Fulfil himself in any other world ? (4.31)

Knowledge, friend, as a sacrifice is greater
Than any other material sacrifice.
For all works culminate at last in knowledge. (4.33)

To know the Truth that saves, you must learn humbly
To bend your knees to the great illuminates,
Then ask them about the Way and lastly, offer
To serve them; then they will reveal to you
The heart of the redemptive mystic knowledge.
The Truth that will deliver you from all falsehood
Whose Light shall enable you to see all creatures
First in your inmost self and then in me,
Even if you are a sinner of sinners you shall

In the boat of knowledge row across the ocean
Of all sins. For this wisdom's great flame burns
The bondage of all action even as fire
Will burn away all fuel into eld.
There's nothing in the world as pure as Knowledge
Which he who attains perfection realises
In the course of time in his illumined soul. (4.34—38)

A man who's anchored to faith and sedulously
Subdues his sense wins to the light of knowledge
Which swiftly leads him to the heart of peace. (4.39)

The ignorant man who has no faith and flounders
In doubt shall perish. For the sceptic has
No anchorage in this world or the next
And so can never achieve true happiness. (4.40)

He who has dedicated all his works
Through Yoga to Him, his doubts dispelled forever,
Can be bound no more by the bondage forged by works. (4.41)

Therefore, rend in your heart with the sword of knowledge
These doubts which stem from ignorance, and rise
To the occasion, upbuoyed by your Yoga. (4.42)

ARJUNA

Thou praisest, Kṛṣṇa, the renunciation of works
And then again belaudest the Yoga of action.
Tell me once and for all — which is the better. (5.1)

KṚṢṆA

Renunciation of action and the Yoga
Of action — both redeem the soul. But the Yoga
Of action is better than that of inaction. (5.2)

He is the authentic yogi who neither desires
Nor loathes anything. Freed from the dualities,
He is delivered swiftly from all bondage. (5.3)

Only the ignorant hold that the Yoga
Of knowledge is other than the Yoga of karma,
Not the wise. For those who practise the one win also
The boons which the other askesis confers. (5.4)

The status attained by the Yoga of knowledge
Is within the reach of those who practise the Yoga
Of action. He who sees no difference
Between the twain may well be hailed as a seer. (5.5)

But without the Yoga of action renunciation
Is hard to attain. The illuminate through action
Wins swiftly the final union with God. (5.6)

He who is trained in the Yoga of works, who is pure
In heart, who is master of his self and has
Conquered all sensual cravings and realised
His identity with every soul can never
Be bound by his action even when he acts. (5.7)

The one who is in union with God knows
That even when he acts he is not the doer,
Whether he sees or hears, touches or smells
Savours or walks, slumbers or breathes or when
He speaks or grasps, opens or closes the eyes.
For he holds that 'tis only the senses which
Act everytime on the objects of the senses. (5.8 — 9)

He who dispassionately does whatever
He undertakes, offering it all to God,
Stays untouched by sin even as the lotus
Remains unwetted even when floating on water. (5.10)

The yogi performs actions merely with
His body, mind, intelligence or the senses
Disowning attachment, to purify himself. (5.11)

The yogi conquering attachment to the fruits
Of works, attains to enduring peace. Those who
Impelled by desire, are attached to the fruit
Of their action do get bound as though by chains. (5.12)

'Tis not the Lord who creates the cycle of works,
Nor makes men feel that they are doers of deeds,
Nor forges the nexus which connects each action
With its results —'tis Nature that works out these ! (5.14)

The Omniprevalent spirit takes not on
The sin or merit of men : 'tis ignorance
That blindfolds knowledge and bemuses all. (5.15)

But those whose ignorance is rent by their knowledge,
Their light, like the sun, reveals the Primal Truth. (5.16)

He whose consciousness is centred in Him,
Whose soul is one with Him, who dwells in Him,
Rapt in His being and whose sins are all
Purged by his knowledge — such a blessed man
Never takes birth again in a human body. (5.17)

The sage views with an equal eye a learned
And humble Brāhmin even as a dog
A cow, an outcaste or an elephant. (5.18)

The ones whose minds achieve equality
Overcome the cosmic world. God who is flawless
Is the same in all. So are those who live in God. (5.19)

He whose intellect is tranquil, and who
Transcends illusions who rejoices not

In things which are pleasant nor feels perturbed when
He's faced by the unpleasant, such a sage
Has realised God and resides in Him. (5.20)

When the sage is not attached to external things
And dwells in God rapt in the bliss of self
Such an illuminate wins everlasting bliss. (5.21)

Sensual pleasures are the source of pain,
For they have a beginning and an end,
So the illuminate cannot rejoice in them. (5.22)

The one who, living a full life, can resist
Successfully the assaults of lust and anger,
Is the authentic yogi and dwells in bliss. (5.23)

The yogi who dwells in psychic felicity
And inner bliss and light becomes divine
And attains to the beatitude of God. (5.24)

The sages who have attained the sinless state,
Who are self-disciplined, delivered from doubts
And vowed to serve all, attain the bliss divine. (5.25)

Those who are disciplined in self and live
In the Soul's light, delivered from lust and anger,
Win through to the beatitude of God. (5.26)

Shutting out all external objects and fixing
His gaze between the eyebrows and his inward
And outward breath moving within the nostrils,
The sage who is intent on liberation
And has curbed his senses, mind and understanding,
Casting away all fear, desire and anger —
Such a sage is delivered from all bondage. (5.27 — 28)

The yogi who has realised me as
The Goal of meditation and the final
Enjoyer of rituals and sacrifice,
Knows me as the Friend of all and attains Peace. (5.29)

Who does the work he is missioned to do,
Not craving for the fruits of his action is
The authentic illuminate and not the one
Who, averse to action, lights not the sacred fire. (6.1)

What people call renunciation is,
In essence, disciplined activity;
For none can be a yogi who has not
Disowned all selfish purpose once for all. (6.2)

Dispassionate action is the means whereby
An aspirant climbs up to the heights of Yoga,
And serenity the means which keeps him poised
On the Yoga's summit once he has attained it. (6.3 — 4)

Let a man redeem himself by his own self,
Nor give in to dejection, for the self
Is the best friend of self, even as the self
Can be its own worst enemy here on earth. (6.5)

To one who has redeemed himself by his self
His self is a friend. To one who has not yet
Known his own self 'twill act even as a foe. (6.6)

He who is a master of himself and has
Attained to harmony stays unaffected
By honour and dishonour, heat and cold. (6.7)

Who realises his self by dint of knowledge,
And remains imperturbable and to whom
Gold and clod and a pellet of stone are one,
Such a man is entitled 'true yogi'. (6.8)

He is the yogi who looks with an equal eye
On saints and sinners, comrades, friends and foes
And all those who are indifferent to him.
Let the yogi always strive to concentrate
His mind on the Supreme — a solitary,
Free from desires, self-controlled, and rid
Of the hankering to grasp at the world's vain laurels. (6.9 — 10)

Serene and fearless, firm in the celibate's vow,
Let him sit with his mind unwavering
And riveted one-pointedly on me. (6.14)

The yogi whose mind is thus controlled, and who
Is poised forever in his mind, abides
In me, having attained the peace of *nirvāṇa* (6.15)

Verily, Yoga is not for the man
Who overeats, nor for him who goes on fasting,
Nor is it for the thrall of sleep nor for him
Who, eschewing sleep, keeps all the time awake. (6.16)

Who's temperate in food and action and knows
How to restrain his craving for the senses,
Who regularly sleeps and keeps awake
To such a man Yoga comes as a healing balm. (6.17)

The man whose disciplined mind is havened in self,
Delivered from all passions and desires,
Such a man is entitled, 'poised in Yoga'. (6.18)

The man who is disciplined in the Yoga of self,
His thoughts controlled by Yoga, such a sage
Can be assimilated to a flame
Burning unflickering in a windless place. (6.19)

In the state when the mind is stilled and is at peace
And one sees with one's self his soul within himself
Know that to be the blessed state of Yoga. (6.20)

That in which you find ineffable bliss
Which is beyond the ken of the senses — but
Can be perceived by the pure intelligence —
Which, realised once, you can nevermore
Forfeit that mystic consciousness which, once
Attained, gives you the certitude that there
Can be no boon greater on earth to be won
And makes you impervious to the deepest pain —
Know that to be the blessed state of Yoga
Which cuts asunder the nexus of all sorrow
It is this Yoga you must practise with firm
Determination and serenity of mind. (6.21 — 23)

Disclaiming vigorously all desires
Born of the selfish will and, holding with
The mind the unruly senses, you must gain
Tranquillity little by little by means of reason
Controlled by steadfast will till, when the mind
Is poised in the self, you abrogate all thought. (6.24 — 25)

The wavering, restless mind goes wandering on
Toward this or that : so you must draw it back
And have it focused every time on the soul. (6.26)

The plenary happiness comes to the yogi whose mind
Is tranquillised and passions are subdued
And who, purged of all sins, attains to God. (6.27)

When the mind is tranquillised and the yogi is
Purged of all sins, and when he constantly
Communes with his soul he enjoys all the time
The beatitude derived from contact with God. (6.28)

The illuminate whose soul is poised in Yoga
And who is equal-visioned sees in himself
All creatures and himself in all His creatures. (6.29)

He who sees me in all and all in me
Can never go out of my sight — no more
Than I can go out of his sight on earth. (6.30)

The yogi who, stablished in the unitive
Experience, worships me in all — abides
In me wherever he may be placed in life
(No matter how he acts he dwells in me.) (6.31)

Who sees everything with an equal eye
As a part of himself, whether in joy or pain,
Such an illuminate is the perfect yogi. (6.32)

ARJUNA

This Yoga of equality which thou
Hast preached to me, in grace, Lord, seems to me
To be lacking in a firm foundation because
Of the innate restlessness of our human nature. (6.33)

For I think it is as difficult to tame
Our strong intractable and restless mind,
As it is to tame the ever-elusive air. (6.34)

KṚṢṆA

Doubtless, friend, the mind is restless and so
Is difficult to tame. One succeeds only
By dint of constant practice and non-attachment. (6.35)

Yoga is an arduous task to one who is
Not lessoned in self-control. But he who is
Master of himself is cut out to arrive
By perseverance and well-directed efforts. (6.36)

ARJUNA

He who cannot control himself and though
He has faith slips up inadvertently,

Failing to win his goal, how does he fare
(Straying from his path thus, on a sudden impulse ?)
And if and when he strays from the Godward path
Shall he miss both this life and the life eternal
As a stray and way-lost cloud dissolves on high ?
Thou must dispel once and for all my doubt
Which none else, Lord, is competent to achieve. (6.37 — 39)

KṚṢṆA

My friend, here or hereafter none who is
A true aspirant ever can come to grief. (6.40)

Having dwelt in the world of the virtuous
For many many years he's born once more
In the house of the affluent and pure of heart.
Or else he's born in an authentic yogi's
Family — but very rare is such a birth. (6.41 — 42)

There he recaptures the predilection of
His past birth (namely, the hunger for the life
spiritual) and thereafter, once again,
He aspires for the deliverance of his soul,
Feeling impelled by the urge of his former birth
As though irresistibly : even a seeker
Of Yoga transcends the world of Vedic rites. (6.43 — 44)

But the yogi who strives assiduously and is
Purged after many lives of his sins, attains
At long last to the highest goal of life. (6.45)

The yogi is greater than the anchorites,
Greater than the man of knowledge, and greater than
The dynamic man of action, so my friend,
Aspire to be a yogi, first and last. (6.46)

Of all the yogis those who, in reverent faith,
Worship me fervently, self-lost in love,
Come closest to my heart, attuned to me. (6.47)

KṚṢṆA

Listen, friend, how by practising the Yoga
With a mind engrossed in me and leaning on
Me as the ultimate and divine ground
You may know me integrally with certitude. (7.1)

I'll reveal to you in full the recondite
Wisdom which, once known, there remains, my friend,
Nothing more to be known here in this world. (7.2)

Among thousands of men only a handful
Aspire to the light and among those who strive
And arrive only a few know me in my essence. (7.3)

Earth, water, ether, fire, air, mind and reason
With the self-sense (*ahaṁkāra*) — these constitute
The eightfold components of my lower nature.
But I have an other, higher nature, friend,
Which is the soul whereby the world's sustained. (7.4—5)

This is the primal womb of all that is
I am at once the world's Source and Dissolution. (7.6)

Nothing is higher than me in the world
I am the thread in which like gems are strung
All, all created things in the universe. (7.7)

In water I am the delectable taste and savour
The light of the sun and the moon, the Veda's Om
Sound in the sky and manliness in man,
The earth's pure fragrance, effulgence of the fire,
The life of all and the ascetic's askesis. (7.8—9)

I am also the eternal seed of all,
The intellect of the intelligent,
The splendour of the stalwart splendid man,
The strength of the strong, reft of desire and passion
And in men the desire that bows to the Law Divine. (7.10 — 11)

And whatever states of being there may be,
Be they harmonious, restless or sluggish
(*sāttvik* or *rājasik* or *tāmasik*)
Know they all stem from me and me alone :
They dwell in me but I dwell not in them. (7.12)

Deluded by these gunas — the three modes,
The world knows me not — the Transcendent and Eternal. (7.13)

Mine is the divine *māyā* of the modes,
Which none can bypass save those who have known me. (7.14)

The wicked fools, low-born in the human scale,
Who are *māyā's* dupes — and feel a kinship with
The demonic temperament — turn not to me. (7.15)

Four types of postulants approach me : first,
Those who are in distress; then those who appeal
To me for boons and favours; third, those who
Are seekers of Truth and, lastly, those who are
The radiant illuminates on earth. (7.16)

Among the ones who turn to me stand out
The illuminates who worship me alone :
I am their hearts' beloved, as they are mine. (7.17)

Noble indeed they all are, but I cherish
Him as my heart's beloved whose soul is linked
With mine and who is havened in me alone,
In devotion, hailing me as the highest Goal. (7.18)

After many a birth the illuminate
Takes refuge in me when he realises
That Vāsudeva, the Lord, is one with all.
But such a great soul is rarely to be found. (7.19)

Men who are led astray by their desires
Appeal to other gods, performing such
Rituals as allure their natures' cravings. (7.20)

In whatever form a devotee may choose
To worship me, I bless and sustain his faith
So it may stay unwavering on his way. (7.21)

Endowed with faith he worships the gods he loves
And wins from them the boons he wants — which, too,
Are sanctioned finally by me alone. (7.22)

Those of little minds crave transient boons :
The ones who worship the gods go to the gods
But my dear devotees come home to me. (7.23)

Men of little understanding do think
Of me, the Infinite Unmanifested,
As human, unknowing my supernal status. (7.24)

Curtained by my own *māyā*, I decline
To reveal my utter Self to all. The bewildered
World knows not me, the Unborn and Sempiternal. (7.25)

I know the past, the present and the future,
But none on earth can divine who I am. (7.26)

All beings are born to delusion, led astray
By the dualities which stem from desire and hate. (7.27)

The virtuous who have attained sinlessness
Are freed from the *māyā* of dualities
And worship me, unwavering in their vows. (7.28)

Those who strive for deliverance from old age
And death to attain salvation when they take
Refuge in me they come to know all about
The spirit's lore, the Godhead and the works. (7.29)

Those who know me along with my Supernal
And material aspects as also the truth.
About me as the Master of sacrifice,
Such souls, engrossed in me, know my divine
Self even when they pass on to the Beyond. (7.30)

ARJUNA

Lord, what is Brahman and what is *adhyātma* ?
What is karma and what is *ādhibhūta* ?
And what are they — *adhidaiva* and *adhiyajña*
Also do tell me how art thou to be known
By the self-controlled when they pass on to the Beyond. (8.1 — 2)

KṚṢṆA

Brahman is the Absolute, Sempiternal
Adhyātma is one's quintessential nature.
Karma is the creative force that brings
All beings into existence. The *ādhibhūta*
Is the mutable basis of terrestrial life. (8.3 — 4)

When the day is done he who his body leaves
Thinking of me alone attains my status
Divine — this you must never doubt, my friend. (8.5)

When a man in his last hour, his body leaves,
Whatever state of being he meditates on
In full absorption that state he'll attain. (8.6)

So at all times remember me and fight
(Do your duty urged by your innate nature)

When your mind and intellect are poised in me,
To me alone you shall come, rest assured. (8.7)

By the discipline of mental concentration
Meditating ever one-pointedly on
The Supreme Divine one can attain to Him. (8.8)

In his last hour, when the aspirant leaves
For the great Beyond, he must think only of Him
Who is subtler than the subtle and whose colour
Is resplendent like the sun. The devotee
Who does this, concentrating steadfastly
All his life-force midway between the eyebrows
With all the resolution and strength of Yoga,
Shall attain the Goal of the Supreme Divine. (8.9 — 10)

There is an imperishable state of which
Knowers of the Veda speak and into which
Those who have attained dispassion enter
And for which mystic celibates aspire :
I will describe to you that state in brief. (8.11)

Closing all the senses' doors and the mind
Withdrawn in the heart, the life-force taken up
Out of its restless movement into the head,
The intellect rapt in the utterance of the Om
And remembering me as he passes away,
He attains after death the highest Goal. (8.12 — 13)

Who are one-pointed and in their hearts remember
Me constantly, attain me easily
And those great souls who have realised me once
And so won the highest status are never reborn
In this ephemeral world, the house of sorrow. (8.14 — 15)

From the high world of God all creatures are
Reborn again and again. But those who have
Attained me reach the point of no return. (8.16)

Those who know that a day as well as a night
Of Brahma lasts a thousand ages, *yugas;*
Are the authentic knowers of day and night.
At the dawn of His day all manifested things
Emerge from the Increate and, at night-fall,
Return once more into the Increate.
These countless beings, who are born ceaselessly
At dawn, merge back helplessly at night-fall,
To be resurrected once more at day-break. (8.17 — 19)

But beyond this unmanifested Entity
There is the Sempiternal Being who
Never can perish even when all else does. (8.20)

This deathless, Increate Superconsciousness
Is my final Abode — those who realise
This Truth, transcend the cycle of rebirth. (8.21)

The Supreme in whom abide all sentient creatures,
And who is Omniprevalent, can be
Attained by single-minded love alone. (8.22)

The yogi, knowing what remuneration
He may win by dint of a study of the Vedas,
Sacrifice, benefactions or askesis,
Bypasses all these virtuous deeds and attains
To the supreme and sempiternal status. (8.28)

To you, who are eligible, I'll now reveal
This profound secret lore illumined with
Wisdom which shall help you to outsoar all evil.
This is the sovereign knowledge, sovereign secret,
To be known by direct experience, beneficent,
Attended with felicity and eternal. (9.1 — 2)

Those who have no faith in this gospel of mine
Shall not attain me and must time and again
Tread the circling track of this death-bound universe. (9.3)

My unmanifested Being pervades this
Universe. All creatures reside in me :
But I do not indwell any of them. (9.4)

As the vast, ubiquitous, untrammelled air
Abides in the sky — even so, know this,
That every creature does abide in me. (9.6)

All creatures at the end of every cycle
Return to my Cosmic Nature. I recreate them
At the beginning of the following cycle. (9.7)

Leaning on my own Nature, *Prakṛti*,
I create time and time again all these
Multitudes of sentient creatures which
Are helpless, being under the yoke of Nature. (9.8)

But these works cannot bind me friend; for I
Preside above them as if indifferent
And unattached to all my cosmic action. (9.9)

Under my aegis Nature, *Prakṛti*,
Gives birth to all things, moving and unmoving
For this reason the world evolves in cycles. (9.10)

The fools look down on me when I assume
The human body, because they do not know
My highest status as the Lord of all. (9.11)

Their actions, hopes and knowledge come to naught
For they feel a kinship with the demonic nature
Which deludes their fool intelligence and will. (9.12)

But the great-souled who dwell in the divine nature,
Knowing me as the eternal source of the world,
Worship me with a single-minded love,
And, pledged to me, bow before me in devotion,
Singing of me day after resonant day. (9.13 — 14)

I'm the father, mother, sponsor and grandsire
Of the world, the goal of knowledge, the pure Om
The triple Vedas — *Ṛk, Yajuṛ* and *Sāma.* (9.17)

I am the Goal, the upholder of all, their Lord
And refuge, friend and ultimate abode,
The fount and basis of the universe,
The divine ground, the imperishable seed. (9.18)

I shed heat, I draw water from the earth
And then send it back once more as the rain,
I am immortality as well as death.
I am, friend, at once Being and non-Being. (9.19)

To those who worship me, meditating on
My utter Self, and who are in constant touch
With me — I grant the boons they have not won
And security in all that they have garnered. (9.22)

Even the devotees of other gods —
Who worship in faith — are, in reality,
Worshipping me, though not in the right way. (9.23)

'Tis I who am the Lord and the enjoyer
Of all sacrifices. But these ignorant men,
Not knowing me, in my essence, stumble and fall. (9.24)

Those who worship the gods wend to the gods,
Who worship the ancestors repair to them,
Who worship the elemental spirits go
To their abode and my own priests come to me. (9.25)

✱ Whatever you offer me in simple love —
A leaf, fruit, flower or even a drop of water —
I accept in love as your heart's dedication. (9.26)

Whatever you do enjoy or sacrifice,
Whatever you give away in charity,

Whatever askesis you undertake
All offer to me in complete surrender. (9.27)

For only then shall you shake off the bondage
Of works with their good or evil consequences
And through renunciation of all attachment,
Achieving liberation, shall commune
With me and finally repose in me. (9.28)

I see all with an equal eye; I am
Attached to none, nor repelled by any man.
I dwell in those who worship me in pure
Devotion even as they, too, dwell in me. (9.29)

Even if a sinner of sinners turns to me
He should be accounted righteous — because
He has entered on the Homeward Path. Aye, he
Shall swiftly be transformed into a saint
And achieve eternal peace. I pledge my word:
My devotee shall never come to grief. (9.30 — 31)

Born to a dismal and unstable world,
You turn to me; focus your mind on me;
Become my loyal devotee and priest,
Bow down before me in love's self-surrender
And dedicate to me your utter self. (9.33 — 34)

Hearken once more, friend, to my supreme word
Now that you respond to me with love,
So you may profit by what I'll reveal.
Gods nor the mighty sages have divined
My Origin. For I am assuredly
The Source of the gods and great illuminates. (10.1 — 2)

The illuminate who knows me as the Lord
Who is unborn and never had a beginning,
Is rendered immune forever from all sins. (10.3)

Intellect, knowledge, truth, self-mastery,
Tranquillity and freedom from illusions,
Non-violence, pain and pleasure, birth and death,
Penury, affluence and equality,
Fear and courage, contentment, charity,
Forgiveness, askesis, ill-fame and fame —
All these states of being derive from me. (10.4—5)

I am the primal origin of all;
From me stem all, the wise who know this Truth
Worship me as such in love's pure ecstasy,
Their minds and hearts centred in me, they dwell
In flawless joy on this one blessed theme,
Day after day delighting one another.
To such dedicated souls who live to love me
One-pointedly, at one with me — I grant
The mind of light so they may come home to me. (10.8—11)

ARJUNA

Thou art the ultimate Divine and pure
Abode, the eternal God of gods, beyond
The cycle of birth — as all the seers proclaim,
Like Nārada, the godly minstrel, Asita, Vyāsa
Or Devāla and thou thyself, too, hast told me.
So I accept all thou hast just revealed.
Demons nor gods have plumbed thy Mystery.
Thou alone, O Supreme Person, knowest Thyself,
O Genesis and Ruler of all that is,
Sustainer of the universe and Leader
Of the destiny of thy creatures in this world.
Do tell me, fully, Lord, of thy divine
Manifestations *(vibhūtis)* whereby thou
Indwellest and pervadest the universe
And how through my meditation I may come
To know thee in my soul. Describe to me

In detail all about your manifestations
In words which rain like nectar from thy lips. (10.12 — 18)

KṚṢṆA

So be it : but I'll only tell you now
Of my major manifestations : for I cannot
Name them all in detail as they are endless.
I preside in the hearts of all : I am
The beginning, middle and end of all that is.
I am Viṣṇu among the Vedic gods (Ādityas)
And among the lights I am the radiant sun. (10.19 — 21)

Lastly, I am the ultimate seed of all
Creatures in cosmos : naught that is immobile
Or mobile, friend, can ever exist without me.
There is no end to my supernal powers.
All I have told you so far is but a brief
Resumé of my multitudinous glory. (10.39 — 40)

Wherever you find an efflorescence of grace,
Opulence, grandeur or power that thrills the heart —
Know : it all derives from a gleam of my sun-splendour.
But I need hardly elaborate it to you
In detail : suffice it that this universe
Is upheld by but a fraction of my Self. (10.41 — 42)

ARJUNA

Because thou hast detailed to me, in grace.
The Supreme Mystery about thy Self,
My clouds of misconception are dispelled.
I've heard, Lord, all about the birth and exit
Of cosmic life and about your mystic greatness.
And I do believe thou art what thou hast
Told me about thy Being. Still I long

To see thy Form Divine, O God of gods !
If thou, O Master of Yoga, deemest me
Eligible for that vision, then reveal
To me thy changeless sempiternal Self. (11.1 — 4)

KṚṢṆA

Behold, my friend, my multitudinous form
In manifold celestial hues and shapes.
Behold the Vāsus, Rudras and Ādityas
And a myriad wonders you have never glimpsed
In my body now behold the whole universe
Moving and moveless and all else you would see. (11.5 — 7)

But you cannot see me with these human eyes,
So I will endow you with the sight divine :
Behold now my celestial Yoga power. (11.8)

SAṀJAYA

With this He, Kṛṣṇa, the mighty Lord of Yoga,
To Arjuna flashed His Sempiternal Form
Of the multitudinous Godhead with mouths and eyes
And vast, breathtaking faces on all sides,
With upraised divine weapons and resplendent
Marvellous ornaments and heavenly robes,
Spraying a celestial soothing fragrance.
If a thousand suns outflashed at once in the sky
Its dazzle might resemble the great Lord's lustre. (11.9 — 12)

There Arjuna beheld the universe —
Countless, divided and yet unified
In one vast body of the God of gods. (11.13)

Then Arjuna, thrilled, his hair standing on end,
Bowed before Him and said, with folded hands : (11.14)

ARJUNA

I see, Lord, in thy body all the gods
And the multitude of creatures along with Brahma
Agleam on his lotus-throne and the heavenly sages
And the numberless celestial serpent-races. (11.15)

I behold thy multitudinous Form with countless
Bellies and arms, faces and eyes, but I see
Nowhere thy end, thy beginning or thy middle,
O mighty continent of the universe ! (11.16)

I behold, in awe, thy crown and mace and discus,
Allwhere glowing whose lustre dazzles the eye :
A mass of flame — ubiquitous, stupendous,
Incandescent and fathomless like the sun ! (11.17)

Thou art the immortal, ultimate Divine,
The Goal of our quest, the final Haven of this
Our universe, the everliving Sponsor
Of the eternal Law, the Primal Person. (11.18)

O thou with no beginning, middle or end,
Endowed with infinite prowess and myriad arms !
Sun and moon are thy eyes, and with thy face
Of blinding fire thou seemst to burn this world. (11.19)

The space 'twixt the earth and heaven and beyond
Is replete with thee, O Lord, and thy gigantic
And terrible Form makes tremble the triple worlds. (11.20)

Innumerable gods, lo, enter thee !
Some, dismayed, sing of thee with folded hands
And galaxies of illuminates and seers.
Apotheosize thee with ecstatic hymns. (11.21)

Hosts of celestial Beings are upgazing
At thee astounded: Rudras, Vāsus, Ādityas,
Sādhyas and Viśvadevas, Uṣmapas and Maruts
Gandharvas, Yakṣas, Asuras and Siddhas. (11.22)

At the sight of thy colossal manifestation
Of eyes, feet, bellies, thighs and numerous mouths,
Horrific with countless tusks, O Lord Almighty,
All the worlds are terror-stricken and so am I. (11.23)

O Viṣṇu, when I see thee impale the sky,
Blazing with manifold hues, with thy mouths agape
And vast flame-eyes, I am a-tremble and peaceless. (11.24)

When I see thy mouths, terrible with their fangs,
Like Doomsday belching fire, I lose my bearings.
I can find no peace, and ask grace of thee,
O God of gods and Refuge of the worlds ! (11.25)

As rivers, in spate, hurtle towards the ocean
Even so these mighty warriors of the world
Rush headlong, Sire, into thy flaming maws. (11.28)

Even as moths plunge into a blazing fire
So the worlds do race into thy gullets of death. (11.29)

Devouring all the worlds on all sides with
The flaming mouths, thou scorchest the worlds with thy fierce
And awful fire, licking them with thy tongues. (11.30)

Do tell me who thou art, O terrible Godhead !
I bow before thee: turn thy heart of grace !
I would know who thou wast from the beginning.
I am ignorant of the will, Lord, of thy workings. (11.31)

KṚṢṆA

I am Time, the grim Destroyer of the world,
And have ordained that all your foes shall die.
Even without you none of these who are
Arrayed against you would survive. Therefore
Arise to win glory, fame and prosperous kingdom
By slaying them. They are slain already by me :
You be now but the occasion — my instrument. (11.32 — 33)

Slay Droṇa, Bhīṣma, Karṇa, Jayadratha
And other mighty warriors as well,
Who are, already, marked as doomed by me,
Nor feel the least compunction, for fight you must
And vanquish these your adversaries in battle. (11.34)

SAṀJAYA

Upon this Arjuna, trembling and dismayed,
Saluted Kṛṣṇa and, with folded hands,
Addressed Him in a half-choked faltering voice. (11.35)

ARJUNA

That the world is entranced by thee, Lord, and delights
In singing thy glory —'tis but meet. Behold
The demons, in terror, flee in all directions
And the bands of illuminates bow down before thee. (11.36)

O resplendent God of gods, greater than Brahma,
The Prime Creator of the world, O deathless
And infinite refuge of the universe !
Who will not bow before thee, Lord, who art
The Being and Non-being and all that transcends them ! (11.37)

O Primal Person and first of the gods, the world's
Supreme cradle, the Knower of all that's known

And the ultimate Goal, with thy multitudinous Self
Thou pervadest the world with thy consciousness ! (11.38)

O Lord of fire and death, wind, moon and waters,
Creator, grandsire and great grandsire of the world !
Hail, hail to thee, a thousand salutations !
We bow before thee, over and over again. (11.39)

Accept our homage, Lord, from every quarter,
O infinite prowess, boundless glory incarnate,
O All-in-all, pervading the universe ! (11.40)

Whatever in flippant jest I may have said,
Unknowing thy divinity, calling in love :
"Come Kṛṣṇa, Yādava, my darling friend !"
Whatever I may have said to thee alone
Or before the others, whatever disrespect
I may have shown thee on the seat or couch,
In play or banquet or lying side by side,
I pray, forgive it all, O Fathomless Ruth ! (11.41 — 42)

Thou art the father of this universe,
Of the moving and unmoving, the Guru of all
And greater than the Guru. In the three worlds
None can ever rival or outrival thee,
O Lord, whose power none can plumb on earth. (11.43)

I bow before thee and prostrate my body
Demanding grace of thee, adorable Master !
Bear with me as a father bears with his son
A friend with his friend, a lover with his sweetheart. (11.44)

I have seen what never was seen before and so
I do rejoice, but my mind is troubled, afraid :
So have thou mercy on me, O God of gods
And Refuge of the world ! O thousand-armed

Form universal ! I long to see again
Thy beneficent human-divine Form,
Dowered with thy discus, mace and diadem. (11.45 — 46)

KṚṢṆA

By my beneficent grace and native power
Of Yoga, I have revealed to you this primal
And effulgent universal Form supreme
Which none before you ever has visioned. Neither
Through sacrifices nor study of the Vedas,
Arduous askesis, rituals or alms-giving
Can this my Form be seen on the human plane.
But be afraid no more, my friend, nor be
Bewildered by my grisly Form. Behold
In peace my genial human form once more. (11.47 — 49)

SAṀJAYA

Thus Kṛṣṇa spoke to Arjuna and resumed
His human form allaying his fears and showing
Himself to His friend in all His grace and beauty. (11.50)

ARJUNA

When I see thee, Lord, in thy blessed human form
I feel reassured and cheerful once again. (11.51)

KṚṢṆA

You have visioned my Form so hard to see :
Even the gods long all the time for a glimpse.
Not through a mastery of the Vedic lore,
Askesis, benefactions or sacrifice
Can one behold what I have unveiled to you :
Only by dint of the soul's one-pointed love

Can you know and see and enter into my essence.
The devotee who lives and works for me,
Forever emancipated from all attachments,
And who bears ill-will to none — attains to me. (11.52 — 55)

ARJUNA

The devotee who, dedicated to thee,
Worships thee and the one who meditates on
The Unmanifested and Ineffable —
Which of these two is more advanced in Yoga ? (12.1)

KṚṢṆA

I hail as my more approved adherent the one
Who worships me with a deep faith and fervour,
Fastening sleeplessly his heart to me. (12.2)

But those who worship the Ineffable
And the Unmanifested Root of all,
The Omniprevalent and Sempiternal,
Such men who, after having curbed their senses,
Judge all with an unbiased intellect,
Dedicated to the welfare of all creatures,
They also, in the end, come home to me.
But those whose minds are constantly set on
The Unmanifested find it a harder task.
For embodied beings must experience great
Difficulty to attain the Unmanifested. (12.3 — 5)

I promptly save from the death-bound ocean of life
Those who dedicate all their works to me
And with an unfaltering ardour meditate
And worship me with their hearts affianced to me.
Centre your mind on me alone and let
Your intellect abide in me — thereafter
You shall ever in my Self dwell, rest assured. (12.6 — 8)

But if, my friend, you fail to rivet your thoughts
On me, then seek to win me by the practice
Of concentration and mental discipline.
If, however, you cannot discipline
Your mind, then do your works all for my sake
(Whose one and only aim is service to me)
For, doing all your works for me alone,
You shall attain the ultimate self-fulfilment.
If you fail to achieve even this, then havened
In me, and renouncing the fruits of all your actions,
Practise the Yoga, master of your self. (12.9 — 11)

Knowledge is superior to the practice
Of mental discipline, meditation is
Superior to knowledge, renunciation
Of the fruits of action is superior
To meditation, leading to lasting peace. (12.12)

Who bears ill-will to none and forgives all,
Who, emancipated from the ego-sense
Of "I and mine", is compassionate and kind,
Who reacts nor to pain nor joy, who's ever
Contented, resolute and master of self,
His mind and intellect focused on me alone —
Such a devotee is near and dear to me. (12.13 — 14)

Who do not ruffle another, nor is ever
Ruffled by others, who is unaffected
By happiness or pain, anxiety or fear, —
Such a devotee is near and dear to me. (12.15)

He who is pure and has no expectations,
Who is unconcerned, untroubled and serene,
Who never presumes to take on things on his own,
Such a devotee is near and dear to me. (12.16)

Who neither grieves nor hankers, neither hates
Nor exults, and who is beyond good and evil,
Such a devotee is near and dear to me. (12.17)

Who sees with an equal eye a friend or foe,
Who stays unmoved by insults or applause,
Suffers from cold nor heat, whom pain nor joy
Can ever affect, who is attached to nothing,
To whom dispraise and eulogy are one,
Who's homeless and yet feels allwhere at home,
Contented with whatever comes his way —
Such a devotee is near and dear to me.
Those who are faithful votaries of this
My immortal gospel and live but for me
I cherish as my beloved devotees. (12.18 — 20)

KṚṢṆA

The body is called the *Kṣetra* and the one (soul)
Who knows it is called *Kṣetrajña*, my friend ! (13.1)

In all Fields I'm the Knower of the Field,
The knowledge of the Field and of its Knower
Is the essence of all true spiritual knowledge. (13.2)

I will tell you now in brief what that Field is,
What are its nature, source and deformations,
What are His powers and what He truly is. (13.3)

It has been hymned by the saints in manifold rhythms,
In a number of inspired poems and also
By the *Brahmasūtra* in reasoned philosophy. (13.4)

The Unmanifested Brahman, self-sense, reason,
The five main elements, senses — ten in number —
The mind and the five objects of the senses,

Desire and hatred, pleasure and pain (these are
The chief modifications of the *Kṣetra*)
Consciousness, collocation and persistence :
These, briefly sum up the Field's deformations. (13.5 — 6)

Disowning of conceit and violence,
Forgiveness, serving the master, purity,
Ingenuousness, steadfastness, self-control,
Humility, indifference to the objects
Of sense, a perception of this earthly life's
Deep limitations — a pointless cycle of birth,
Disease and sorrow, petering out in death —
Non-attachment to the home and family
Looking with an equal eye on pleasure and pain,
Unwavering devotion to me, the Lord,
Turning to solitude far from the din
Of crowds, deep aspiration for the lore
Of the soul and a seeking of spiritual Truth,
All this is the authentic knowledge — and what
Is at variance with it is ignorance. (13.7 — 11)

I will tell you now of the knowledge that will lead
To immortality : 'tis the Supreme God,
Beginningless which neither is nor is not. (13.12)

With His hands and feet, His eyes, ears, heads and faces
Spread allwhere, He dwells in all, enveloping all. (13.13)

He appears to have the qualities of all
The senses and yet He is devoid of them.
He is unattached and yet contains the world,
He is bereft of the modes of *Prakṛti*.
And yet is the enjoyer of them all. (13.14)

He is outside and withal, inside all creatures;
He's static and dynamic, unknowable

Because of His infinitesimal subtlety;
He is far-off and yet so close to us all.
He is undivided and yet seems to be
Divided endlessly in all His creatures.
He is known as the sustainer of all that is
Creating and destroying time and again. (13.15 — 16)

He is the Light of lights beyond the darkness,
Knowledge, the pathfinder and the goal of knowledge,
The eternal Resident of every heart. (13.17)

So I have told you briefly about the Field,
Knowledge and what has to be known. Who is
My devotee wins to my status when
He knows this. And you have to know, besides,
That *Prakṛti*, and *Puruṣa* are both
Beginningless. This, also, you must know
That from *Prakṛti* stem the forms and modes,
And the chain of cause and effect is forged by
Prakṛti (Nature) who creates and acts
Puruṣa (the Soul) enjoys the pleasure and pain.
The *Puruṣa* enjoys *Prakṛti's* modes.
Attachment to these triple modes is the cause
Of the *Puruṣa's* birth in good or evil wombs.(13.18 — 21)

The Lord in the body is said to be the Witness,
The Permitter, the Upholder, the Experience. (13.22)

He who thus knows Nature, the *Prakṛti*
And Soul, the *Puruṣa* — if and when he acts
He does not return to earth to be born again. (13.23)

By meditation some envision the Self
By the lone self ; others by dint of knowledge,
Still others by means of (dispassionate) action. (13.24)

Yet others, ignorant of these paths of Yoga,
Hearing about Him worship Him — they, too

Win immortality — harking in their hearts
To the great message of the Spirit's call. (13.25)

This, too, know that wherever a being is born,
Moving or moveless, stems from the union
Of the Field and the knower of the Field, my friend. (13.26)

He is the true seer who sees the Supreme
Presiding equally in the hearts of all,
Imperishable when all else perishes. (13.27)

As he sees the Lord equally everywhere
He does not let his self be harmed by his self
And so attains to his supernal status. (13.28)

He is the seer who sees that all our acts
Are done by Nature and so he is not the doer. (13.29)

When he sees that the multitudinous states of men
Stem but from One and are projected from
Him alone — such a seer realises God. (13.30)

As this Supreme Imperishable Self
Is beginningless and transcends the qualities
(The triple gunas — *sattva, rajas* and *tamas*)
So even when He indwells in the body
He neither acts nor gets involved, my friend. (13.31)

As the all-pervading sky because of its rare
Subtlety can never be tainted by
What it contains — even so every soul
Remains immune though it pervades the body. (13.32)

As the world is manifested by the sun
Even so the soul manifests the entire body. (13.33)

I will again reveal the Supreme Knowledge,
The highest man can win — whose light has led
The sages to inviolate perfection.

Under the aegis of this Knowledge they
Evolve till when they are one with my own nature,
They are born no more at the dawn of cosmic life,
Nor dismayed by the Night of dissolution. (14.1—2)

Mahad-Brahma is the womb, wherein I cast
My primal seedling whence are born all creatures.
(*Mahad-Brahma* and *Prakṛti* are identical) (14.3)

Whatever beings are born from any womb
Mahad-Brahma is their Primal Mother and I
Their Primal Father who inseminate her. (14.4)

Sattva, rajas and *tamas* are the triple
Gunas or modes of Nature (*Prakṛti*),
Which hem the soul in the prison of the body. (14.5)

Of these the *sattva*, because of its purity
Is bright and taintless — still it binds by its cords
Of attachment man to knowledge and happiness. (14.6)

Rajas — the vital energy — attracts
By its lure of craving and desire and thus
Thralls man by his attachment to life and action.
Tamas (inertia) stems from ignorance,
And enslaves man by its urge to indolence,
Somnolence and negligence in all things. (14.7—8)

Sattva attaches man to felicity,
Rajas to action, and *tamas* to sloth
By veiling wisdom's beneficent light. (14.9)

Sattva prevails when it curbs *rajas* and *tamas*,
Rajas prevails when it curbs *sattva* and *tamas*,
Tamas prevails when it curbs *sattva* and *rajas*. (14.10)

When knowledge outwells through the senses' gates,
You may conclude that *sattva* is dominant. (14.11)

The urge to action, restlessness, desire
And greed predominate when the *rajas* rules. (14.12)

Inertia, darkness, negligence, delusion —
These predominate when *tamas* prevails. (14.13)

Virtuous actions which derive from *sattva*
Entail felicity, *rajas* ends in pain
And *tamas* brings in its train but ignorance. (14.16)

Sattva engenders knowledge, *rajas* — greed,
Tamas — delusion, ignorance, negligence. (14.17)

When the seer sees none other than the modes
As the doers, and knows the One beyond the modes,
Then he attains to my supernal status. (14.19)

When one transcends the modes he passes on
Beyond the ambit of mortal destiny
Of birth and death, old age and pain, and wins
The eternal bliss of immortality. (14.20)

ARJUNA

What are the distinctive signs of the man who has
Risen above the (gunas) modes in life
What is his way of life and how does he
Transcend the triple gunas, tell me, Lord ! (14.21)

KṚṢṆA

One who transcends the modes looks not with disfavour
The light of *sattva*, activity of *rajas*
And the delusion of *tamas* when they prevail,
Nor misses them when they have ceased to be.
He sits unconcerned, not driven by the modes
And stands unwavering because he knows
That things are done by the functions of the modes.

Poised in his self he sees with an equal eye
Sorrow or joy, a clod or pebble or gold :
The unpleasant and the pleasant are one to him.
Throned in tranquillity, dispraise or praise,
Honour or dishonour affects him not.
When two parties go to war with neither he sides
As a partisan, nor is he eager to take
An initiative in action on his own.
Such a man is said to have risen above the modes. (14.22 — 25)

Who worships me with an unfaltering love
Transcends the modes forever and becomes
Eligible for the union with God.
For I am the Divine Ground the foundation
Of eternal dharma and immortal life and bliss. (14.26 — 27)

They speak of the eternal *Aśvattha* tree,
Rooted in heaven whose branches lean to earth.
Its every leaf is a psalm of the Vedas : he
Who knows this truth the Vedas' secret knows. (15.1)

Its branches extend both upward and downward,
Nourished exuberantly by the modes,
Its leaves are objects of the senses and roots
Reach earthward ever impelling men to action
(Stemming, in the last analysis, from desire).
It real nature or form can never be known,
Nor its beginning, terminus or foundation.
So with the ruthless axe of non-attachment
One must hew away this strong firm rooted tree
And seek the status of the Primal Being—
Pledged to seek asylum in Him alone—
Who is the ageless genesis of all action
And initiative and once you merge in Him,
The soul is never born again in the world. (15.2 — 4)

Those who are freed from egoism and delusion
And, having conquered the evil of worldly attachment,

Have turned, once for all, to the Spirit's call,
And, subduing all desires have passed beyond
The dualities of pain and happiness,
Attain the state which is beyond all change. (15.5)

The status which once attained delivers one
From the compulsion to return to earth
Is my eternal Being which neither sun
Nor moon nor fire ever can reveal. (15.6)

A part of my Eternal Self is born
In the world as creatures and draws to itself
The mind with the five senses, dwelling in Nature. (15.7)

When the Blessed Lord assumes a body and then
Leaves it for another He takes with Him
The senses and the mind and onward fares
Like the wind which carries the pollen of the flowers.
He uses the ear, the eye, the sense of touch
And taste and smell and enjoys His cosmic play,
When He leaves or stays rejoicing in the body
In contact with the modes; the purblind fail
To vision Him, but those who have attained
The blessed eye of light can see it all. (15.8—10)

The true aspirants striving earnestly
Find Him in their own hearts. But all those who
Are unconscientious and impure can never
Behold Him even though they go on striving. (15.11)

The splendour of the sun which lights the world
And the lustre of the moon and fire are mine. (15.12)

I dwell in all hearts, memory stems from me
As well as its loss. I am the One to be known
By the Vedas even as I am the Author
Of the Vedānta and the Knower of the Vedas. (15.15)

The are two kinds of (*Puruṣa*) Entity
In this universe — the mortal and the immortal,
(The *Kṣara* and the *Akṣara*). Things which are
Created (known as *Kṣara*) are perishable :
The increate (the *Akṣara*) never can perish. (15.16)

But the highest *Puruṣa* is other than these :
He is the Supreme Everliving Lord,
Who sustains and permeates the triple worlds. (15.17)

As I transcend the mortal and even the immortal
(*Kṣara* and *Akṣara*) I'm known in the Vedas
And the world as the Supreme (*Puruṣottama*). (15.18)

Who, free from delusion, knows me as the topless
Reality loves me with all his soul. (15.19)

I have revealed to you this starry secret :
He who once realises this, my friend,
Attains the highest fulfilment in the world. (15.20)

A man born with the divine nature is
Fearless, simple and pure, a votary
Of the Yoga of knowledge, generous, master of self,
A student of the scriptures. He practises
Hard askesis and offers sacrifices.
He is ingenuous, truthful, free from anger,
Tranquil in mind, serene, unmarred by malice,
Gentle, forgiving, peaceful, strong, not fractious,
Greedy, haughty or hypersensitive. (16.1 — 3)

A man born with demonic nature is
Conceited, arrogant, choleric and harsh. (16.4)

The divine endowments lead to liberation
And demonic proclivities will lead to bondage.
But you, Arjuna, need have no misgivings,
For you are born with a destiny divine. (16.5)

Two types of beings are to be found in the world:
(*Daiva*), divine and (*āsura*), demonic
I have described to you about the former
In some detail, now hear about the latter. (16.6)

Those who are born with a demonic nature
Know neither the truth about the way of action
Nor of renunciation. They know not truth,
Purity or right conduct. They proclaim
That this is a dark godless world of falsehood,
Based on no moral law, where all the creatures
Are conceived in lust and born of copulation. (16.7—8)

With this outlook these perverts do wrong actions,
Lost souls of little understanding, they come
As enemies of the world to destroy all. (16.9)

With insatiable pride and full of deceit,
Arrogant, drunk with pride and self-importance;
They run blindly after what is despicable
And all the ends they foster are unclean. (16.10)

Plagued by numberless cares which cannot come
To an end except at death, they hold that life's
Summum bonum is sensual enjoyment.
So, bound by a hundred chains of hope, they become
Helpless puppets of anger and lust and strive
By dishonest means to go on hoarding wealth. (16.11—12)

"I wanted this and have gained it today.
I covet that and will have it tomorrow.
This wealth is mine already and I shall win
Tomorrow that as well. I have done to death
This enemy, the other, too, I'll slay.
I am a lord enjoying life, on velvet,
Happy and strong, a rich aristocrat.
Who can compete with me ? I'll sacrifice
To the gods, give alms and revel in the fleshpots,"—

So they vaunt and rant, dupes of their ignorance,
Led astray by their wrong thoughts, embroiled in
The snare of their delusion, these deep addicts
Of sensual joys fall into a foul hell. (16.13 — 16)

Arrogant braggarts, inflated by their wealth's
Purblind intoxication, they sacrifice
To the gods only in name, not in the way
Approved of saints but bound by shackles of pride
And lust and wrath they castigate me, the Lord,
Indwelling in themselves even as in others. (16.17 — 18)

In the cycles of life and death these evil-doers
And malignant creatures I cast time and again
Back into the wombs of degraded beings;
So these lost souls, reborn to demon darkness,
Birth after birth come not back home to me,
But roll down into hell inexorably. (16.19 — 20)

Three are the gates to this perdition, the death
Of the soul : the gate of lust, the gate of wrath
And the gate of greed. Therefore beware of these. (16.21)

When a man bypasses these three gates of darkness,
He does what leads in the end to the soul's salvation
And enters the path of the supreme fulfilment. (16.22)

But he who flouts the commandments of the scriptures
And is driven by his lusts, can never attain
Happiness or the soul's summit perfection. (16.23)

So be guided by the scriptures' findings when
You want to know what's right and what is wrong :
Aye, you must follow their lead whenever you act. (16.24)

ARJUNA

O Kṛṣṇa, those who do not consult the scriptures
And yet sacrifice to God on high, sustained

By faith — what is the nature of that faith ?
Is it *sāttvik, rājasik* or *tāmasik* ? (17.1)

KṚṢṆA

Faith among human beings is of three kinds :
'Tis either characterised by *sattva* or
By *rajas* or by *tamas* — in accordance
With his fundamental temperament. Now listen :
A man consists of the faith he comes to cherish.
So whatever his faith is — he becomes that.
The *sāttvik* worship the gods, the *rājasik*
Worship the overlords of power and wealth,
The *tāmasik* deify the jinns and ghouls. (17.2 — 4)

Know those men to be of demonic nature
Who mortify their flesh persistently
In ways not sanctioned by the scriptures ; these
Fools torture the vital powers and me, the Lord,
Who dwell in their bodies. They are by and large,
Impelled by lust, conceit and cruelty. (17.5 — 6)

People of *sāttvik* nature like foods which
Conduce to their longevity and increase
Their vitality, health, energy — and which are
Savoury, soothing, succulent and healing.
Men of *rājasik* temperament like foods
Astringent, bitter, sour, salty, hot,
Pungent and acid — in a word, foods which cause
Distemper of the mind and body. And those
Who are *tāmasik* like foods which are impure. (17.8 — 10)

A sacrifice is *sāttvik* when its urge
Derives from a sense of duty — when 'tis offered
In accordance with the scriptural injunctions.
But when it is performed for ostentation
Or vainglory—it is inspired by *rajas.*

And when 'tis offered against the holy law,
Without faith or gifts of food or hymns of worship,
It is known as a *tāmasik* sacrifice. (17.11 — 13)

Worship of gods and gurus, sages, Brāhmins,
Ingenuousness, non-violence, cleanliness
And sexual purity — all this is known
As the askesis of the body. The utterance
Of words which give no offence, words which are good,
To speak the truth that heals but does not hurt
And regular study of the sacred books —
All this is known as the askesis of the speech.
The practice of serene simplicity,
Gentleness, silence, purity of thought
And self-control — is the askesis of the mind. (17.14 — 16)

This threefold askesis practised with one-pointed
Faith by men without any expectation
Of reward or recognition is known as *sāttvik*.
Rājasik is that askesis which is practised
With loud conceit to be worshipped or applauded
By men — even though the joy is transient.
Tāmasik is that askesis which is practised
With the cruel motive of harming others or
The perverse satisfaction of self-torture. (17.17 — 19)

That gift is *sāttvik* when 'tis given at a proper
Time and in a fit place to one who is
Truly deserving — not because of past
Benefits or in expectation of
A future recompense but simply because
The giver feels 'tis right for him to give. (17.20)

That gift is *rājasik* when it is given
In expectation of a like return
Or reluctantly or with a selfish motive. (17.21)

Tāmasik is that gift which one accords
Contemptuously to an unworthy person
At the wrong time and in the wrong place, without
Regard for the feelings of him who receives it. (17.22)

Om Tat Sat — these three words symbolise God,
From whom in the beginning were created
The Vedas, Brāhmins and the sacrifices. (17.23)

And so of old the hierophants of God
In the scriptures enjoined men to intone Om
Before a sacrifice, gift or askesis. (17.24)

And with *Sat* (the Absolute) those who aspire
To liberation initiate various acts
Of giving, askesis and sacrifice,
Not expecting remuneration for their deeds. (17.25)

Sat also connotes reality, existence,
Even as goodness and praiseworthy acts. (17.26)

Sacrifice, askesis, giving alms or deeds
Offered to God — these also are called *Sat*.
But if one performs an act of sacrifice,
Offers a gift or turns to askesis,
Not centreing his faith and will in God
Then 'tis vain (*Asat*) in this world or hereafter. (17.27—28)

ARJUNA

Lord, please explain to me the difference
Between *Saṁnyāsa* or renunciation of works
And *Tyāga* or non-attachment in the world. (18.1)

KṚṢṆA

The sages hold that the repudiation
Of all acts motivated by desire

Is renunciation (*saṁnyāsa*) and the disclaimer
Of the fruits of action is (*tyāga*) non-attachment. (18.2)

Some say: "All action ought to be eschewed
As an evil." Others hold: "Nay, none should ban
Askesis, benefactions or sacrifice." (18.3)

So my final conclusion is this, my friend :
That askesis, benefactions and sacrifice
Should not be banned, for these do purify
The wise — so one must do these as his duty,
Without desire or attachment to their fruits. (18.5—6)

Renunciation of a prescribed duty
Is a wrong movement : such a repudiation
Through ignorance is known as *tāmasik*. (18.7)

He who shuns a duty because of fear
Or the pain it causes never shall profit by
His renunciation — which is *rājasik*. (18.8)

But when one performs an action sanctioned by
The scriptures, urged by a sense of duty, with
No attachment or desire for its fruit,
Such a renunciation is called *sāttvik*. (18.9)

A *sāttvik* illuminate who is free from doubts
And attachments neither longs to do what is
Agreeable nor shrinks from acts which are
Disagreeable. It is not possible
For an embodied being to abstain
Altogether from works. He who renounces
The fruits of all his works achieves true *tyāga*. (18.10—11)

Threefold is the fruit of the works of one
Who has not renounced the fruit of action — namely,
Pleasant, unpleasant and a melange of both,
Which shall be duly reaped in the next world — but

Those who are free from all desire shall not
Be bound by the chains of their acts here or hereafter. (18.12)

The Sāṁkhya doctrine holds that all works spring
But from five causes. Let me tell you of them :
The arena of action, the body, the doer, the means
Of perception and the will of Providence.
Whatever one does with his body, word or mind
Is occasioned by one or the other of these. (18.13 — 15)

This being so, the man with a perverse mind,
Who, thanks to his little discernment, looks upon
His soul as the doer of action, sees awry. (18.16)

He who is free from the ego-sense and whose
Intellect is not clouded even if he
Comes to slay his enemies is not a slayer
Nor is he bound (by his act of slaying them). (18.17)

Knowledge, the object of knowledge and the knower —
The trio constitute the mind's impulsion
To action. Also, there's another trio
Which make all earthly action possible :
The instrument, the action and the doer.
The Sāṁkhya says : the doer, knowledge and action
Are of three kinds classed by the difference
In the modes. I will describe now what they are. (18.18 — 19)

The knowledge whereby one beholds the unique
And imperishable Being in all becoming —
The Undivided One in disparate things —
That integral knowledge is known as *sāttvik.*
That knowledge in whose half-light one beholds
Different beings in multifarious creatures
(Missing their basic common unity)
That knowledge is to be known as *rājasik.*
That narrow and ignorant knowledge which can never

Envision the true nature of the world
And clings forever to one single movement
Equating it with the whole — is *tāmasik*. (18.20 — 22)

An action which is rightly regulated,
Performed without attachment, like or dislike,
With no eye for the fruit — is known as *sāttvik*.
But the action done by a boasting egoist,
Desire-impelled, with an excessive strain,
Is *rājasik*. And the action undertaken
By one who is driven by a deluded spite,
In disregard of his own capacity,
Or the loss he may sustain — is *tāmasik*. (18.23 — 25)

That man is *sāttvik* who is free from the gyves
Of egoism and attachment, who is zealous
And unaffected by success or failure. (18.26)

Rājasik is the man who is passionate,
And seeks the fruit of his works, who is impure
Malevolent, greedy and swayed by joy and pain.
The doer who is fickle, indolent, uncultured,
Procrastinating, stubborn, vulgar, deceitful,
Malicious and despondent is *tāmasik*. (18.27)

Sāttvik is that wise intellect which knows
The truth about the basic urge to action
Even as of abstention — and also knows
Which actions are commendable and safe
And lead to liberation and which are wrong
And dangerous and deliver one to bondage. (18.30)

Rājasik is that intellect which blunders,
Unknowing what is right and what is wrong,
What is spiritual and what is not. (18.31)

When the consciousness is clouded by ignorance
And mistakes what is right for wrong and sees
Everything awry 'tis *tāmasik.* (18.32)

A man's firmness (*dhṛti*) is entitled *sāttvik*
By virtue of which through the Yoga's concentration
He masters his vital energy, life and senses. (18.33)

The steadiness whereby one holds fast to duty,
Lucre and pleasure and desires the fruit
Of every action of his is *rājasik.* (18.34)

The obstinacy wherewith a fool refuses
To be rid of indolence, depression, grief,
Repining and vanity is *tāmasik.* (18.35)

And now, friend, I will tell you of three kinds
Of happiness one may win through a tranquil
Determination until all one's pain
Is abolished. Know that happiness as *sāttvik*
Which tastes at first like poison but, in the end,
By a self-understanding, tastes like nectar.
That happiness is *rājasik* which, stemming
From the touches of the senses with their objects,
Tastes like nectar at first but ultimately
Repels like poison. Lastly, *tāmasik*
Is that happiness which both at the beginning
And at the end deludes the soul because
It springs from somnolence, sloth and negligence. (18.36 — 39)

There is none on earth or in heaven among the gods
Who is free from these three modes of *Prakṛti.* (18.40)

The works assigned to Brāhmins, Kṣatriyas,
Vaiśyas and Śūdras are graded in accordance
With the qualities born of their inner nature. (18.41)

Serenity, self-mastery, purity,
Spirituality, forbearance, wisdom,
Askesis, ingenousness — all these
Are known as the Brāhmin's natural attributes. (18.42)

Heroism, prowess, steadiness, skilfulness,
Largeheartedness, in battle dauntlessness,
Administrative ability — all these
Are a Kṣatriya's natural attributes. (18.43)

Trade, commerce, agriculture and tending cattle
Are a Vaiśya's natural duty, even as
Serving men through work is a Śūdra's duty. (18.44)

A man attains salvation when he cleaves
To his own vocation. Let me explain to you
How he achieves this when he does his duty. (18.45)

The One who pervades the universe and is
The origin of the compulsive urge to action —
When Him men worship with their works, assigned
By him as their duty they attain perfection. (18.46)

Better is an action prompted by your nature —
Even if it is not done well — than the one
Well done when 'tis another person's duty,
But not your own. You incur no sin when you
Do your duty that suits your temperament. (18.47)

None must disown a work hailed by his nature,
Even when 'tis defective. For all work
Is dogged by defects even as fire by smoke. (18.48)

The person who has achieved non-attachment,
Self-mastery and conquest of desire,
Through renunciation wins the supreme state
Of self-fulfilment which transcends all action. (18.49)

Now listen, I will briefly tell you, friend :
How, having achieved perfection, one attains
God — the last pinnacle of aspiring knowledge. (18.50)

Led by a pure intellect, steadily
Mastering oneself and turning away from
Din and objects of sense, casting aside
Attraction and loathing, courting solitude,
Eating but little, gaining full control
Over body, speech and mind and constantly
Meditating and taking refuge in
Dispassion, tranquillity, disowning all
Desire and anger — and, delivered from
The possessive instincts and the ego, one grows
Worthy of communion with the Lord. (18.52—53)

One who communes with the Godhead grows serene.
He neither grieves nor craves, but looking with
An equal eye on all that lives, attains
Deep love for me in the light of which he knows
My multitudinous divinity
And what I am in essence and thereafter
He penetrates into my Being's core.
Then, whatever he does, taking refuge in me,
Through my deep grace he wins the eternal Abode. (18.54—56)

Offering all your actions to me you must
Regard me as your Goal and then, led by
The Yoga of understanding, constantly
Fasten your thoughts on me to be one with me. (18.57)

When you are one with me you shall, friend, cross
All your hurdles. But if from egoism
You decline to heed me then you shall be lost.
If in your fool conceit you still declare
"I will not fight"— vain shall be your resolve :

Your nature shall appoint you to the task,
For you yourself have forged your *karma's* chains
Whereby you are bound. So you'll be driven to do
What in your ignorance you now wish to shirk. (18.58 — 60)

The Lord indwells the hearts of all whom He turns
Round and round as if mounted on a machine
By His *māyā*. Turn to me in every way
Of your being and you shall come to the supreme
Peace and the everlasting Abode of Rest. (18.61 — 62)

Now that I have revealed to you the wisdom
Which is the secret of secrets, I enjoin you
To ponder it fully and then act as you will. (18.63)

My well-beloved friend ! now hearken to this
My Word supreme — the saviour Secret which
I will tell you for the welfare of your soul. (18.64)

Become my-minded, my lover and adorer,
A sacrificer to me and bow before me
And I pledge my word, for you are dear to me,
That you shall, in the end, come home to me.
Abandoning all codes of conduct (dharma)
Take refuge in me alone and from all sins
I will deliver you, have no misgivings. (18.65 — 66)

But tell not this to one who scoffs at me
Or one who is not a devotee or one
Who is loath to listen or one who never harks
To the Spirit's call. But the man who in his heart
Loves me and explains to my devotees
This inviolate truth shall surely attain to me.
None among men can serve me better than he
And there is none on earth I cherish more. (18.67 — 69)

Now tell me, dear friend, have you absorbed all
I have revealed to you ? Have you seen daylight
Which quells the abysmal darkness of ignorance ? (18.72)

ARJUNA

My doubts and misconceptions are all gone,
Lord, by thy grace. I will now do thy will (18.73)

SAṀJAYA

Such was the thrilling duologue I have heard
Between the Blessed Lord and His great disciple. (18.74)

King ! everytime I recall the marvellous
And sacred duologue between Lord Kṛṣṇa
And Arjuna — I rejoice again and again ! (18.76)

Where Kṛṣṇa the Lord and Master of Yoga presides
With Arjuna, the archer, there must prevail glory,
Prosperity, victory and swerveless dharma. (18.78)

Thoughts on the Gita

In life we feel constantly at a loss when confronted by the disturbing question: how to know which is the way to Truth, the road to the gleaming Goal beyond our vale of tears and shadows? In other words, where is the starting point and which is the direction that leads to the final liberation from our labyrinth of mists and shackles of flesh ? Correct answers to such pointed questions are of primary importance because if we make here a false start we are bound to land ourselves in a quandary, straying away farther and farther from the right orientation. In Sri Rup's *Padyāvalī* there is a pregnant Sanskrit quatrain indicating the progressive gradations of true Yoga of which the first three lines are :

ādau śraddhā tato sādhusangoṭha bhajanakriyā
tatonartha-nivṛttiḥ syāt tato niṣṭhā rucistataḥ
athāsaktis-tato bhāvastataḥ premābhyudancati

That is to say, there are nine major stages or milestones in the soul's progression towards the Destination, the Journey's end :

1 *śraddhā,* faith ;
2 *sādhusaṅga,* consorting with holy men ;
3 *bhajanakriyā,* spiritual self-discipline or askesis ;
4 *anartha-nivṛtti,* the overcoming of the obstacles that come in the way ;
5 *niṣṭha,* indomitable determination to follow His lead of light;
6 *ruci,* finding an incipient pleasure in plodding on ;
7 *āsakti,* the pleasure deepening into joy ; or, shall I say, savouring what seemed dry for years ;
8 *bhāva* alias *bhakti,* devotion ;
9 *prem,* devotion ripening into ecstatic God-love.

Some hold *prem* as synonymous with *mahābhāva,* the celestial lotus which outpetals on the stem of *bhakti.* Many a sage has said that *prem* or *mahābhāva* is lasting *bhakti,* others describe *prem* as the crowning fulfilment, the ultimate goal of Yoga. But in as much as such deep questions cannot be decided by dint of definitions which must, in the last analysis, seem either academic or speculative, let us have for our goal either *bhakti* (devotion) or *prem* (love) as the soul's ultimate haven of fulfilment.

(Ramakrishna was wont to say that *prem* or *mahābhāva* can be realised only by the *Iśvarkoṭi*, the born yogi. The *jīvakoṭi*, or the average aspirant, can only realise *bhakti* and feel utterly fulfilled thereby).

The Gita holds that faith leads an aspirant through the light of knowledge to the heart of Peace (4.39) and that the clue to faith (or knowledge) can be had only from the illuminates, *tattvadarśīs*, to whom one must first and foremost learn to bow in all humility (4.34). For only an attitude of humility can make our aspiring intellect receptive to the light of knowledge or spiritual wisdom. The modern mind loves to take its stand on the much-vaunted self-reliance. The courage of standing on one's own feet or, shall I say, the vibrant claim to be the architect of one's destiny is not scotched by the Gita. Kṛṣṇa blesses it as manliness in man (7.8), about which I will have more to say in due course. But here the aspirant must be forewarned against the pride (which does not stem from manliness or courage but from our innate obstinate egoism) which says : "I can't accept anything on trust and insist on seeing or knowing prior to believing or accepting." Such an attitude may sound sonorous but is intrinsically hollow in that it leads in the end to utter barrenness. Ramakrishna, king of similes, was wont to say that the haughty peaks may look resplendent but are seldom arable — it is the valleys and plains where water can collect that bear fruit and yield corn. The self-sure reasoning intellect's claim to be the final arbiter of the spirit's findings cannot but lead to sterility of the heart because the light of the Spirit is and must always be utterly beyond the ambit of the judicial intellect. In the world of the Spirit the aspirant has to accept first — that is, hold fast to faith — before he can come to know or see. Apropos, I may quote here a letter, my guru, Sri Aurobindo wrote to me because it is germane to my theme. He wrote, commenting on a rationalist's strictures on faith:

"As a matter of fact there is no universal infallible reason which can decide and be the umpire between conflicting opinions; there is only my reason, your reason, X's reason, Y's reason multiplied up to the discordant innumerable. Each reasons according to his view of things, his opinion, that is, his mental constitution and mental preference. So what is the use of running down faith which after all gives something to hold on to amidst the contradictions of an enigmatic universe ? If one can get at a knowledge that knows, it is another matter : but so long as we have only an ignorance that argues — well, there is a place still left for faith — even, faith may be a glint from the knowledge that knows, however far-off, and meanwhile there is not the slightest doubt that it helps to get things done. There's a bit of reasoning for you : just like all other reasoning, too, convincing to the convinced but not to the unconvincible, that is, to those who don't accept the ground upon which the reasoning dances. Logic, after all, is only a measured dance of the mind, nothing else..."

I give this long excerpt from Sri Aurobindo's letter because it underlines the standpoint of faith or the psychic values as against the rational-mental. One of the most difficult hurdles a spiritual aspirant has to cross in life is this gulf between the awards of the logical mind and the perceptions of the intuitive soul.

To give an instance in point, the Gita holds (5.18) that an illuminate looks with an equal eye on an enlightened Brāhmin, an outcaste or an animal. The logical intellect can hardly be expected to endorse such an absurd view. But the vision of the psychic being does very often seem queer if not crazy to our mental preconceptions not to mention prejudices. As a matter of fact one of the major difficulties of an aspirant on his pilgrimage to the unknown is the bewilderment caused by the clash between his conventional mind's humdrum notions of right and wrong and the soul's startling glimpses of truth and light. The case of Arjuna in the Gita's very first chapter is an instance in point. Many an intellectual feels a moral kinship with his view (2.5) that even living by begging is preferable to bloodstained enjoyments of a royal victory. A noble-hearted man feels strongly the horror of shedding blood, the more so if his opponents happen to be — like Arjuna's — his friends or relatives. But Kṛṣṇa met the qualms of his disciple's conscience with arguments from two angles. First, from the social which puts a premium on duty : that is, it is incumbent on one who is born to the warrior caste (*kṣatriya*) (2.31-32-33), to follow his svadharma,[1] secondly, from the spiritual point of view which holds that the question of killing cannot really arise, since the soul, being immortal, can neither kill nor be killed (2.20-21-22).

And her Kṛṣṇa presents an interesting fact to ponder on, the more so because it is so original. He says that a man's life is visible only in the middle (2.28) he was non-existent before his birth and reverts to non-existence after death. Therefore why attach much importance to life which is so transitory ? One is reminded forcefully of the great poet-saint Ramprasad who assimilated life to a mere bubble :

jaler bimbo jale udoy jal hoye se mishai jale

That is :

A bubble erupts and floats awhile
Upon the rippling river
And then, lo, it dissolves again
Into the stream for ever !

Nonetheless Kṛṣṇa exhorts Arjuna to follow the line and lead of his svadharma and adduces convincing arguments to initiate him with the mantra of action as against inaction, courage as against cowardice, the philosophic attitude as against the sentimental jeremiad. And his most flaming hortatory reproach is (2.3) :

Klaibyaṁ mā sma gamaḥ pārtha, nait t'at tvayy upapadyate

That is :

Do not yield to sentimental cowardice, because it is unworthy of you, and disown once and for all this lachrymose faintheartedness : you must needs rise to the occasion.

It is to be noted that Kṛṣṇa chided Arjuna to instill into him His own divine energy (as the best antidote to the attack of dejection fathering faintheartedness) because the latter, groping in his labyrinth of darkness, had thrown himself utterly at Kṛṣṇa's feet, accepting Him as his Guru and Pilot, appealing to Him in deep dejection (2.7) :

Afflicted with the weakness of self-pity, my Lord, and with my mind in a turmoil, I see no way out. So in this blind darkness do flash thy lead of light to me, thy disciple, I seek refuge in thee.

And Kṛṣṇa responded with alacrity with a loving affirmation, accepting him as his friend, disciple and agent rolled into one. For he needed his ward no less than the ward needed his guardian.

Otherwise He could not perhaps have flung at him the flaming reproaches He did. For it is incumbent on the guru, should the occasion arise, to confront his disciple with home truths. Ordinarily, we fight shy of such vehemence because criticism, still less castigation, often works the wrong way as sighed the sage Vidur in the *Mahābhārata* :

Apriyasya ca satyasya vaktā śrotā ca durlabhaḥ

That is :

Rare is the speaker who utters home truths
As is the auditor who profits thereby.

But in an authentic guru-disciple relationship there must be perfect frankness which brooks no compromise or partition — for he is no true master who tactfully spares his disciple even as he is no true disciple who disobeys his master's injunction rebelliously. So neither did Kṛṣṇa hesitate to reprimand Arjuna nor Arjuna decline to be spurred on by His divine indictment to do His will. And Kṛṣṇa had to scourge Arjuna in order to waken his drooping energy and latent righteous indignation which, once roused, can work miracles. For Kṛṣṇa was no ordinary guru any more than Arjuna was an ordinary disciple. Had not the divine Friend assured His human suppliant previously (*Mahābhārata, Udyogaparva*):

Yastvām dveṣṭi sa mām dveṣṭi yastvām anu sa mam anu

That is :

Who hates you, in effect, hates me as well.
Even as he who loves you loves me, friend !

In the Gita Kṛṣṇa insists that faith is the starting point for the pilgrim of the spirit. But how to have faith ? There are indeed a few blessed souls to whom faith comes as spontaneously as the laughter of light with the morning sun. But to the vast majority faith comes generally after a deep and protracted struggle and heartache, and life appeals because of its superficial glamour and *joie de vivre*. To the child everything seems wonderful and exciting — unless of course its natural evolution is dammed and desires get thwarted. But it dawns on us all, little by little, that things are not what they seem and that we are swayed by forces over which we have no control, down-pulls which oppose at every turn our innate idealism and natural evolution towards the light. That is why the human aspirant voiced thousands of years ago the vibrant prayer (*Bṛhadāraṇyaka Upaniṣad*):

Asato mā sad gamaya
Tamaso mā jyotir gamaya
Mṛtyor mā amṛtam gamaya

That is :

Lead me from the unreal to the Real,
Lead me from darkness to Light,
Lead me from death to Immortality.

But whence uprises this eternal prayer ? — From the heart of faith which attests the Unknown sustained by an inextinguishable intuition which even when enveloped by blind darkness knows that there is a Sun denied by the evidence of dusk and clouds, a victor Light which must ultimately erase the darkest midnight of the soul, a mystic bliss which can heal all pain, an Empyrean of Grace vowed to uplift us from the abyss of doom to the peak of immortality.

Yes, this faith is there lying latent in every soul, only by the Yoga of aspiration the dormant fire has to be awakened, the unstrung notes to be woven into a melody, the lonely seeds to be nurtured into a flowering fulfilment, the slough of despondence to be traversed resolutely.

But how can this incredible miracle be achieved ?

The Gita gives a helpful answer — helpful because Kṛṣṇa is not an addict of pious platitudes which sound sonorous but lead nowhere. So he says that the only way to move towards the light is to seek the help and blessings of the illuminates who live in light.

But all who approach such radiant teachers do not pray for the highest boon the soul thirsts for. There are broadly four types of aspirants, says our Blessed Lord (The Gita, 7.16) :

Caturvidhā bhajante māṁ janāḥ sukṛitino'rjuna !
ārto jijñāsur arthārthī jñānī ca bharatarṣabha !!

That is :

Four types of virtuous men approach me : there are those who are in distress; those who appeal to me or the gods for boons and favours; those who are real seekers of Truth and, lastly, those who are the radiant illuminates on earth.

Obviously, Kṛṣṇa here implies a gradation of consciousness :

1 The *ārta* is the common man in distress who turns to the Divine even as an ailing patient does to the doctor to obtain relief or cure.

2 The *arthārthī* or the suppliant, he is not a derelict, but is ambitious or just a greedy petitioner who wants to exploit the Divine as a stepping-stone in order to climb on to a higher plane of affluence, power or fame or simply for the fleshpots.

3 Next comes the Truth-seeker whose approach must be ranked higher because he is impelled by a superior urge to seek the Divine —an urge not of his flesh, craving for comfort or luxury, but derived from a psychic thirst to know what most men ignore because they take life as they find it with no real ache to delve deeper beneath the surface appearance of things. So, naturally, he moves a step closer to the heart of Truth and Light of Divine Grace.

4 Lastly, comes the illuminate, the *jñānī,* who has received a substantial modicum of Light from direct experience of the diamond beams of the spirit which entitles him to the coronet of the *jñānī.* It is to be noted, however, that this *jñānī* is not yet a *siddha mahātmā* who is stationed on the peak of light and bliss but is just one who is sustained on the peak of light and bliss but is just one who is sustained by the Divine Grace in his pilgrimage to the Everestian summit-vision, the Divine Beatitude. He is simply an illumined soul who treads the sunlit path, vowed not to pause or rest on the way till he arrives at the feet of the *Puruṣottama,* the Supreme bridge-builder between the Manifest (*Kṣara*) God and the Unmanifest (*Akṣara*) God where in a luminous restfulness one sees a thrill that :

All that is, shines by His Light [2]

and so is acclaimed Kṛṣṇa as one of the blessed elect (7.17) proclaiming :

Teṣām jñānī nityayukta ekabhaktir-viśiṣyate

That is:

> *Among the ones who turn to me stand out the great illuminates who worship me alone, because I am their heart's Beloved, even as they are mine.*

Kṛṣṇa, even as the sages before and after Him, proclaims over and over again that at the summit of mystic love, *bhakti* and *jñāna* (love and knowledge) merge into each other and shine almost like two facets of the same Realisation. A great Yogi has said : "He who says he knows but does not love does not know and he who says that he loves but does not know does not love."

One hears often mystics declaring that on the way to the summit the rhythm of the devotee, *bhakta*, may indeed differ from that of the illuminate, *jñānī*, but once one climbs to the summit — or even the higher plateaus of mystic experience — the line of demarcation between the two looks like a reed dividing the water of a pond, so that one gets rid, willy-nilly, of man-made definitions which would tend to keep apart the *bhakta* and the *jñānī* in separate water-tight compartments. That is why Sri Ramakrishna said that what he actually experienced on the Yoga's path did not tally with what he had heard about it from others who had described to him as of the essence of Yoga.

But to come back to the main question : how to know which path would suit one's temperament — or in the Gita's terminology : what is one's svadharma — the native line of evolution which leads to the ultimate fulfilment ?

To this question Kṛṣṇa has given us in the Gita a very categoric answer : He says to Arjuna, His beloved disciple : (4.34)

tad viddhi praṇipātena paripraśnena sevayā
upadekṣyanti te jñānaṁ jñāninas - tattvadarśinaḥ

That is :

> *To know the saviour Truth you must first learn to bow to the great illuminates ; then ask them about the way and lastly, offer to serve*

them, for then they'll reveal to you the heart of the mystic and redemptive knowledge.

It is to be noted how unambiguously the Teacher of the Gita gives an answer of light to the questioning heart groping in darkness. The three steps are :

1 You must approach the illuminates humbly if you really want to know about the bliss and fulfilment that light alone can bring in its train. It is plain commonsense. For who else but the man who has lit the mystic fire (*agni*) in his heart can undertake to teach us how to shelter it with infinite pains and vigilance from the gusts of doubt and storms of denial till it finally deepens into a conflagration which can hold its own against the blackest winds. But an infant cannot achieve what only the adult can with all the strength that accrues to him from life's trials and tribulations. One aches for the divine light and yearns for the divine love because without them life remains a catacomb of dismal darkness. From the moment the child is born it stands in need of light and air, love and guidance. Its parents, nurses and guardians have to guide and educate it with infinite patience in order to teach it how to cope with the ways of the world and learn at every step how to grow and aspire to the heights which alone can ransom the prisoned life of day by day enringed by the granite walls that stand between the pilgrim and the goal. What its parents and teachers do on the physical-mental plane the illuminates do on the psychic-spiritual.

2 Thereafter he must ask questions, as Arjuna does, (*pariprasna*) about the nature of the Divine Light and how to attain it.

3 Last, though not least, he must offer to serve the illuminates, his gurus, for only through service to them can one grow to greet them with love. This is necessary as love alone can teach one how to open the windows of one's psychic being to the Light Divine which needs an opening to stream through and irradiate the darkness, the only Light that can dower the lonely soul with flowering fulfilment and authorise it to claim :

vedāhaṁ etaṁ puruṣaṁ mahāntaṁ
ādityavarnaṁ tamasaḥ parastāt

That is :

I have known the Sempiternal Being
Resplendent like the golden sun
Who, stationed beyond the night of the soul,
Presides o'er His dominion.

So men have hailed these seers as the supreme teachers, the day-bringers who have eluded the clutch of life's darkling siren, māyā. Why this māyā of make-believe was created has been discussed and thrashed out thread-bare by countless saints and seers down the ages. Kṛṣṇa does not give a clear-cut answer. He simply states (7.14):

daivī hy eṣā guṇamayı mama māyā duratyayā
mām eva ye prapadyante māyām etāṁ taranti te

That is :

This divine māyā too is mine and acts in a triple mode on the phenomenal world in a way which none can elude save those who, taking refuge in me, bypass its siren clutch.

The three modes (gunas) are *sattva, rajas* and *tamas* about which Kṛṣṇa had a great deal to say but intended primarily for those who tread the path of *jñāna*, knowing that devotees (*bhaktas*) generally are not vitally interested in such philosophical and metaphysical questions. In India the doctrine of māyā and the three gunas has been written, argued and speculated about for centuries by the illuminates, savants and commentators. But although Kṛṣṇa was to throw subsequently a world of light on these three modes. He had at this stage other fish to fry which he looked upon as far more important. For example, He had to enlarge on action, knowledge, equality of mind, acceptance of the reality of avatarhood, loyalty to the spiritual values, the resplendent powers of Divinity (*vibhūtis*), the tragic clinging of the multitude to their fool ignorance fostered by their egoism, their doubts and fears, perversities and vacillations and lastly, the supreme message of devotion (*bhakti*) the marvellous solvent of all din, discord and disharmony.

Indeed, He elucidates with a brilliant profundity recondite mysteries but only to hark back time and again to the breathtaking illumination of love and the necessity of dispassionate action which,

He holds, one must on no account disown even though all earthly action is, like everything else in an evolving cosmos, essentially imperfect. This momentous question He explains with an ingenuity as masterly as it is convincing : to wit, how action can liberate and why it binds, but emphasises everytime that though dispassionate action must help us onward and purify the heart[3] the ultimate Goal can be attained best and quickest through *jñānamiśrā bhakti*, that is, love guided by knowledge. For instance, he says to Arjuna (6.47):

yoginām api sarveṣāṁ madgatenā 'ntarātmanā
śraddhāvān bhajate yo māṁ sa me yuktatamo mataḥ.

That is :

Among the various yogis I hold the ones as closest to my heart — who, in true faith, worship me fervently, self-lost in love.

And again: (8.22)

puruṣah sa paraḥ pārtha bhaktyā labhyas-tv ananyayā
yasyā 'ntaḥsthāni bhūtāni yena sarvam idaṁ tatam

That is :

The Supreme in whom abide all sentient creatures and who pervades the universe can be attained only by single-minded love.

I will have more to say on this theme dear to the Lord's heart, but before that I feel I should answer a modern question which constantly vexes the mind of the so-called freethinker who wants to break all idols.

The revolt of an iconoclast stems, in the last analysis, from his ego and ignorance of the spiritual values and the psychological necessity of eager humility (especially for a spiritual seeker). That is why he bridles as soon as the sadhu — and still more the guru — appears on the horizon. What he says in effect boils down to a sturdy refusal of his intellectual pride which declines to bow to the will of a teacher who can teach only when one accepts his lead in humble reverence. What the rationalist says, in effect, is that he cannot accept the evidence of another being, and depends utterly on the lead of his own experience, and self-confidence sponsored by the supreme arbiter Reason which fulminates : "*Tattvadarśī*, the illuminate ! Pooh ! Why should he presume to be an intermediary through whom alone God's Grace can be conveyed ? Why should not the devotee claim manfully that he is well-equipped from birth to seek the Light of lights which alone can ransom our cribbed and cabined life from its dismal cell ?"

The answer to such haughty questions is that Kṛṣṇa's ratification of the authority of the spiritual men to guide us seekers home is based on the realisation of thousands of helpless aspirants the world over that one who does not know the nature of the mystic Reality should, in his own interest, approach those who have known it, for the simple reason (attested by history) that only those who have seen the Light can win to the authority with which their vision endows them. Knowledge is power not only in the realm of science and learning but in the domain of mysticism as well. The aspirants who have not attained the eye of light cannot help, still less guide, those who are athirst for Light. The Vedic seer warned the seeker of light against the grave danger of following a false prophet who, boasting a twinkling intelligence, is utterly at the mercy of the flail of ruthless Fate. From the mystic's point of view such a prophet is as good as blind and so, they must come to grief who, pining for vision, are led by blind leaders since the blind cannot lead the blind.[4]

We have seen that Kṛṣṇa, who is love and wisdom incarnate, came to accept Arjuna as his disciple as soon as he accepted the God-man as his guru. But to boon with the eye of light an evolved being like Arjuna — who is a fighter as well as a seeker — is not an easy task because one question asked by such a wide-awake soul must lead to another which in its turn leads to a third which is by no means easier to answer trenchantly without reservations. So Kṛṣṇa had to go all out to convince Arjuna that what seems magnanimous from the sentimental point of view may be in reality as blameworthy from the spiritual viewpoint as the attitude of an escapist who wants to follow the lead of his sentimental-vital or logical-mental being as against that of the soul's perceptions and intuitions. Time and again He flashed His gleaming compass in answer to Arjuna's call for light in his labyrinthine gloom of ignorance. With infinite patience He presented to his bewildered devotee the standpoint of an authentic Yogi as against that of a sentimental greenhorn whose emotional turmoil incapacitates him to appraise rightly the spiritual values. That is why Kṛṣṇa had now and again to repeat Himself— to drive home His point from different angles to win Arjuna over to the way of the illuminate as against that of a supercilious rationalist or a feckless sentimentalist. At the same time He assured his confounded friend that though Truth is one, the paths that lead up to its golden portals may very well be different for different pedestrians. A few instances may serve to make my meaning clear.

Arjuna asks Kṛṣṇa (12.1) :

> *Among those, Lord, who in unwavering faith worship thee, whom dost thou favour most ? Thy devotees whose call springs from the heart or those who prefer to meditate on thy unmanifested and ineffable self?*

To which Kṛṣṇa answers (12.3.4.5) :

> *I favour those who worship me with the heart's deep faith and fervour. But those who meditate on the Ineffable and Unmanifested Divine and, after having subdued their senses and judged all with an unbiased mind, are dedicated to the welfare of all creatures, they also in the end come home to me. Only those whose minds are centred in the Unmanifest (Akṣara) God find it a harder task because it is difficult for an embodied being to realise the (Akṣara) Godhead.*

Kṛṣṇa had to stress the importance of the heart's lovelit worship of the Divine incarnate in a form because in His time — and before His advent too — the illuminate (*jñānī*) alone used to be panegyrised even by eminent Yogis. The devotee (*bhakta*) also had, indeed, a place among the seekers but their status was not nearly as high and impressive as that of the illuminate who was hymned by the rank and file in awed reverence. The devotee was looked upon merely as a *nimna adhikārī* — that is, one who is not eligible for the higher boon of knowledge by identity, *nirvikalpa samādhi,* where duality is abrogated — knowledge, the known and the knower being all rolled into one because of the soul's mergence in the Formless *Akṣara* Godhead. The intransigent feud between the pilgrims of the two paths — the *jñānamārgī* and the *bhaktimārgī* — is a very ancient one. In a nutshell, the former strives to go beyond the mind by silencing all flickers of thought, *cintā,* while the latter transcends the mind through the comparatively simpler — and less arduous — childlike devotion of a loving surrender.

It has been often asked by readers of the Gita why on earth should a follower of the Yoga of knowledge — which Kṛṣṇa repeatedly indicates by the name sāṁkhya — look down on a votary of devotion. The answer is not difficult to find. Those who are made of the sterner stuff — the stalwart aspirants — feel a deep yearning to prefer the difficult to the easy path. The votary of devotion fights shy of askesis, that is, austerity for austerity's sake. Not so the votary of knowledge who does often feel an inordinate pride to traverse the more arduous path. To climb a mountain becomes even more thrilling when the ascent is difficult and dangerous. The heroes would naturally want to achieve heroic feats, holding that what is not beset with perils, is hardly worthwhile — what makes the blood tingle, what many attempt but only a handful can accomplish is the laurel of laurels. The sagas and epics electrify the blood because of the raptures of the dangers they deal in. "It is a happiness to wonder" says the poet. And what can be more wonderful than a pilgrimage to the trackless heights ? The illuminate is built of the intrepid stuff of the colossus. So let us bow to him, a king among men.

The argument is not altogether invalid. The rare pearls do not float on the surface. One has to dive deeper and deeper till they can be culled from the depths difficult to reach.

Only one thing : the illuminate may not have erred in thinking that he is called and chosen to achieve what the lesser fry dare not even dream of. But the devotee's hurdles, too, are not easy to cross. For none who is not vowed to stake his all for the All-in-all can possibly direct all his energy along a single channel, and surrender his pride at the Lord's feet and say with the spirit and flesh made one: "I seek refuge in Thee alone. Thou comest to transform my wan clay into a lotus-garden — I promise to do Thy will and however stubbornly my self-will may rebel, I will make Thee my one idol and accept gladly whatever Thou ordainest ; even when I do not see Thy hand I will not flinch no matter if I become a complete derelict because I have full trust in Thee although I have not glimpsed Thee so far."

Is such a love's surrender a whit less difficult than the grand and aloof meditation of the illuminate on the Formless Divine, the *Akṣara* Godhead ?

Nevertheless, alas, the Lord's full approval of the way of devotion has been misunderstood by the *jñāna-mārgīs.* They have said in effect that Kṛṣṇa had to prescribe not only for the elect but for all and sundry who are not cut out to follow the thorniest and steepest path to the highest peaks, so for them a tincture of genial and complacent *bhakti* has been sanctioned. Has he not asserted categorically (4.37-38) that as fire burns all fuel into ash even so the flame of knowledge reduces all action into cinder and that there is nothing on earth as pure and holy as knowledge.... and so on and so forth.

But such exegeses are essentially tendentious. No wonder ever so many commentators have read into the Gita what they want to, arguing down with wordy eloquence all other interpretations as invalid.

I dub such commentaries 'tendentious' as the votary of action, too, may cite chapter and verse vindicating his view that the Gita is a gospel of action — ceaseless action — (3.8, 3.19, 3.20,...) others may cite as cogently couplets vindicating the viewpoint of devotion (11.54, 14.26, 18.55...)

But this is not the correct way to interpret the Gita's teaching nor the best way to profit by its serene harmonious wisdom, as has been pointed out by Sri Aurobindo in his masterly *Essays on the Gita* in which he has hailed Gita's gospel as essentially a synthesis, that is, a triune path reconciling with marvellous profundity the three approaches of *jñāna, bhakti,* and *karma* which alone can lead up to the vision of the Supreme *Puruṣottama* beyond the *Kṣara* and *Akṣara* God.

The Gita's message of the *Puruṣottama* is truly a resplendent one. It would be presumptuous on my part to try to explain it in intellectual terms as the *Puruṣottama* is a Light beyond all lights, an Entity beyond all entities, a Superconsciousness beyond all consciousness, an inconceivable Presence beyond the cosmic (*Kṣara*) and the extracosmic (*Akṣara*) who builds a bridge between the personal and the impersonal aspects of the Divine. So suffice it to say that without this grandiose Presence the discrepancy between the manifest and unmanifest would vex the devotee's consciousness for ever. It may be assimilated to the vault of the sky joining the East to the West. Without the *Puruṣottama* the human consciousness would seem adventitious — an unsolved discord and as there could be no convincing vindication of *karma* or earth-life, the illuminate would be justified in his summary dismissal of all action as a play of inexplicable māyā. It is because this *Puruṣottama* exists — the Supreme Personality beyond all human personalities — that the Divine descends into the cosmos as an *Avatāra*. For if *Puruṣottama* were non-existent the cessation of action and mergence of all creaturely consciousness back into the Unmanifest (*Akṣara*) Godhead would be the final and rational end of life — the consummation devoutly to be wished — because life would then cease to have any meaning or purpose and therefore the votary of exclusive *jñāna* would be more than vindicated in branding all action as suspect. "Why all this pother," he would say, "when you can lie ensconced in the 'Peace that passeth all understanding' ?" Also, the descent of the Divine into the heart of life to redeem it would make no sense. For why should He want to be born on earth to redeem it from "age to age" (4.8) (*yuge-yuge*) for the protection of the sadhus and chastisement of the wicked and why in the name of good sense should He want restoration of Dharma on such a waylost and fortuitous planet which is always flickering, trembling and precarious ?

"No," says the Lord categorically in the Gita, "my birth and action are essentially divine" (4.9) and adds : "I do pervade the cosmos and from me stems the primal urge to ceaseless action which, once accepted in the right spirit, leads to the final fulfilment of life (18.46).

It is to lead distracted life through a progressive evolution of unconsciousness that His *Līlā*, cosmic play, started in creation aeons upon aeons ago — though this is necessarily, a speculation since none can say whether this play of life ever had a beginning or will ever have a denouement.

But we need hardly come to a definite decision on this impenetrable mystery. Besides, why vex our puny consciousness with such unanswerable questions — when we can see, if we really want to, that life though an enigma is also a joy where even pain can hand us over to a Finale whose glorious diapason we do feel reverberating in our bones — as is borne out by the master-minds of all climes : the poets, prophets and *avatāras*. So why not let ourselves go, dancing on the purling rapids of love and light, joy and rapture, thrill and wonder ? For life despite its limitations does thrill us and drive us ever on whither we know not — but does it matter ? — since we can and do feel the touch of the Divine by doing His will ? Is it not glorious enough in all conscience to feel that He answers our aspirations and descends to mould us to His will ? The Gita testifies to such rapturous revelations at every turn. What can possibly matter thereafter — when we can experience in every tingle of our blood (*Sāvitri*, 2.6) :

Even grief has joy hidden beneath its roots,
For nothing is truly vain the One has made,
In our defeated hearts God's strength survives,
And victory's star still lights our desperate road!

This great message of the Gita has been attested by Sri Aurobindo as that of the *Puruṣottama*.[5]

The Supreme is the Puruṣottama, eternal beyond all manifestation, infinite beyond all limitation by Time or Space or Causality or any of His numberless qualities and features... He is the Supreme transcendent Spirit and all comes into manifestation from Him and are all His forms and His self-powers... He is the eternal Master of all manifested existence, Lord of the worlds and their creatures... He is in all and all are in Him : He has become all and yet too. He is above all... He is the transcendent Divine; He descends as the Avatāra; He is manifest by His power in the Vibhūti; He is the Godhead secret in every human being. All the gods whom men worship are only personalities and forms and names and mental bodies of the one Divine Existence.

It has been asked by many a seeker of Divine Truth how could one possibly profit by such hearsay evidence of a Supreme Entity who chooses mysteriously to transcend not only the manifest Cosmic Divine but the unmanifest extracosmic Godhead as well. Kṛṣṇa has answered the question trenchantly saying (15.19) that one who, after rending the cosmic māyā, has visioned Him as the Supreme *Puruṣottama* "adores Him in every way, heart and soul." He has left it at that, leaving the seeker to realise its momentous corollaries. For in the world it is not easy to give oneself heart and soul to the Divine. Even those who are advanced Yogis fail to surrender themselves without reserve at the Lord's feet, because first of all, the Lord immanent in the world — the Cosmic Divine — seems somehow bound by the limitations of life, and then, in the second place, in His Extracosmic Existence (*Akṣara* Entity) He seems too grand and fabulous to be hailed as a friend, as Arjuna so pathetically apologised to Kṛṣṇa (11.41-42). That is another reason why the Lord had to assume His Supreme Personality as the *Puruṣottama*, where His grandeur does not outrule intimacy — on the contrary He greets us all-too-tenderly as a Supreme Personality, thus utterly erasing our over-whelming fear by the nectarous touch of His incredible Grace. For one must bear in mind that Kṛṣṇa revealed His *Viśvarūpa* to Arjuna not to appal him. He flashed out the superhuman and fantastic magnificence of His all-embracing divinity only to make thereafter His humanity all the more delectable by contrast as it were. That is why Arjuna, when he all but lost his bearings, had to appeal to Kṛṣṇa to resume his "serene human-divine form" *saumyaṁ mānuṣaṁ rūpaṁ*. Kṛṣṇa complied, but after having transformed Arjuna's consciousness by according him a fleeting glimpse of His *ne plus ultra Puruṣottama* Personality which at once transcended and harmonised both the personal and impersonal aspects of the Supreme Godhead.

I have made mention of Kṛṣṇa's approval of svadharma indicating a vocation. But He does not stop there. He builds on it and adds (4.13) that the fourfold order — of Brāhmin, Kṣatriya, Vaiśya and Śūdra — was created by Him in accordance with their native capacities and aptitudes.

Sri Aurobindo's luminous and comprehensive commentary on this dictum is elaborated in his *Essays on the Gita*. (Chapter entitled, "Svabhāva and Svadharma.") I can append here only two brief excerpts:

"The fourfold order was created by Me," says Kṛṣṇa 'according to the divisions of quality and active function'. On the mere strength of this phrase it cannot altogether be concluded that the Gita regarded this system as an eternal and universal social order. Other ancient authorities did not so regard it; rather they distinctly state that it did not exist in the beginning and will collapse in a later age of the cycle. Still we may understand from the phrase that the fourfold function of social man was considered as normally inherent in the psychological and economic needs of every community and individual existence."

What Sri Aurobindo means by this he explains lucidly : "There are thus four kinds of works, the work of religious ministration, letters, learning and knowledge, the work of government, politics, administration and war, the work of production, wealth-making and exchange, the work of hired labour and service. And endeavour was made to found and stabilise the whole arrangement of society on the partition of these four functions among four clearly marked classes. The system was not peculiar to India, but was with certain differences the dominating feature of a stage of social evolution in other ancient or mediaeval societies. The four functions are still inherent in the life of all normal communities, but the clear divisions no longer exist anywhere."

In other words, men are not born equal, having different aptitudes and talents, inclinations and proclivities. Ramakrishna loved a song in which occurs a line :

Kāre dāo Mā, Indra-pada — kāre karo adhogāmi

That is :

Some you, Mother, coronate and some consign to hell.

Large-hearted men naturally have protested in chorus against such a dispensation, branding it all as fostering favouritism, cruelty and injustice. But do what we will, men and things in nature *are* born at different stages of development to fulfil different functions. All herbs do not have medicinal properties, all trees do not grow to lofty heights, all rivers do not purl or dance, all hills do not reveal snow-ranges of breathtaking beauty. In fact it has been contended by some of the greatest philosophers that life would be intolerably dull and boring if all men were of the same stature, born with equal strength or capacity. In Canto 10, Kṛṣṇa enlarges on the theme of *vibhūti* which He sums up thus (10.41): "Wherever you find an outflowering of grace, strength or grandeur that thrills the eyes you may infer that it all derives, from a gleam of my effulgence."

One is hardly impressed by the banal, common or mediocre. As a matter of fact when one looks at the world with the realist's eye one cannot help but conclude that mediocrity serves more or less as a foil to greatness. Anything precious is rare — such is the law of life, as has been emphasised by Kṛṣṇa in His vindication of the golden peaks manifesting His divinity as against the humdrum plains where mists and shadows abound.

The question has been asked whether the Gita's is a gospel meant only for the elect as against the common man. The answer was given by the Lord categorically in His advocacy of equality — *samatā*. Equality is the essence of Yoga, so much so that an aspirant cannot win to the status of seerhood till he has grown to "see with an equal eye the learned and modest Brāhmin, the cow, the elephant, the dog and the outcaste." (5.18) None but a seer can vision a truly divine light emanating not only from all and sundry but the outcaste and the lower animals as well.

Which however must not be misinterpreted, for seeing the divine light in all creatures does not mean that the light emanating from the animal is nearly as bright or splendid as the light outwelling from a great *vibhūti*, a radiant personality. Kṛṣṇa's startling finding (6.29) that he who is equal-visioned everywhere sees himself in all and in himself does not imply that every manifestation on earth has the same stature, girth or splendour. The sentimentalist often forgets this truth and claims that since all are sons of God therefore all must be hailed as equally great. Such a contention — though foolish and untenable — has been proclaimed by many a muddled thinker who has grievously travestied the Gita's profound and mystic philosophy of equality, *samatā*. But those who have had a true vision have in all ages acclaimed Kṛṣṇa's vision of the world evolving sleeplessly toward greatness calling us all to the heights as one of the most uplifting messages uttered by Him, an exhortation that is based on His assertion that though He exists in all, He manifests His light more in the perfect and the great than in the flawed and the mediocre. To give but a few instances as He puts it in Canto 10:

> *Among the rivers I am the Ganga, among the mountains the Himalaya, among the seasons the spring, among the animals the lion, among the weapons the flail of thunder, among the rich Kuver, among the*

progenitors Kandarpa (Cupid), among the sages Vyasa, among the titans Prahlāda...

I refrain from explaining the proper names as that would necessitate diving into our vast mythology. So I will now take up the thread where I left off, to underline what is really meant by *sva*dharma and how on its basis the superstructure of the four castes has stood for thousands of years.

Kṛṣṇa said (3.35) : "It is wiser to follow a line of evolution consonant with one's innate nature, svadharma — even when it is imperfect than to tread with a faultless gait a path alien to one's native temperament." And He goes on to elaborate it in the last Canto (18.48): "It is better to do what is prompted by your nature even if it is not done well — than to do admirably what is somebody else's svadharma." He might well have left it at that but evidently He thought that He had not been emphatic enough and so repeated: "An action that is acclaimed by your nature should not be left undone even when it cannot be done flawlessly because when all is said and done all action is essentially marred by its native limitations even as fire is by smoke."

Could one be more categoric ? No, Kṛṣṇa is nothing if not helpful, emphatic, and luminous. The Divine can hardly afford to be vacillating and vague. So let us accept it as Kṛṣṇa's succinct dictum that a man's self-realisation can be best achieved when he accepts the native urge of his svadharma.

Therefore, He explained (4.13), He classed men into four castes basing the division on the law of svadharma :

1 The Brāhmin, whose svadharma is to master the lore of the spirit and follow the call of the higher intellect.

2 The Kṣatriya, who rises to his highest stature when he answers the call of his nature to rule his state and, when war is incumbent on him, to fight and chastise the wrong-doer.

3 The Vaiśya, whose role is trade, agriculture and production of wealth, exploiting the natural resources of the land.

4 The Śūdra, the menial or labourer — in modern political terminology, the proletariat — whose svadharma is to serve the higher castes.

The tenet that each of these four types should follow his native svadharma does mean that a Brāhmin should aspire to be an illuminate, a Kṣatriya to be a ruler or warrior fighting for justice, a Vaiśya to be a producer of wealth, trader or a merchant, and a Śūdra to be of service to all.

It has been claimed by many a profound thinker and philosopher that the caste system as it obtained of yore (not as it prevails today) did derive from a divine origin and so gave Hinduism the marvellous resilience and stability which have endured through ages, meeting the challenge of waves upon waves of ruthless Hūṇas and soulless vandals. Nonetheless the modern mind cannot help but feel repelled, in particular by the heartless exploitation of the have-nots of the lowest caste, the Śūdras. How can one possibly defend the Brāhmins' dogmatic branding of the Śūdra as congenitally ineligible for the higher studies and nobler vocations when the history of human experience testifies so often to a low-born outcaste soaring to eminence on the twin wings of industry and genius ? In other words, the argument in favour of the caste system cannot be acceptable to us today if its champions plead that it is inviolable and hereditary. For none can overlook with impunity the irrefutable fact that in ancient India men in the four castes were not held intransigently — on the ground of heredity — in water-tight compartments. No living and progressive society can afford to ignore the just claim of a native talent, not to mention genius. A statesman who declines to foster exceptional capacities of gifted citizens is blind because he cannot see that a nation or community becomes stagnant and reactionary in which the purling waves of delightful talents subside into a tragic stillness. But obviously, as everybody cannot be exceptionally gifted, one may well claim that classing men into four castes was not, on the balance, an unjust or arbitrary dispensation of Providence. For men *are* divided broadly into these four castes all over the world. And as the proof of the pudding lies in the eating thereof, the advocates of the caste system may well claim that it was, on the whole, justified since it did prevent Hinduism from disintegrating for long millennia.

So, what is to be deprecated is not the caste system as formulated by Kṛṣṇa but the rigidity — the following after the letter of the scriptural injunctions (forgetting that 'the letter killeth but the spirit giveth life') a pernicious habit which so often mars man's natural evolution. What Kṛṣṇa outrules is *varṇaśaṁkara* that is an unthinking mixing up of the four castes, bringing in its train either an arid and imposed uniformity or sheer confusion. In other words, the Lord enjoined Arjuna to act out the part of the loyal Kṣatriya, the rich role assigned to him by Providence. A man born to nobility, He says, is duty-bound to behave nobly. *Noblesse oblige.*

Which does not mean that one must elevate the doctrine into a rigid dogma or shibboleth. When in ancient India dharma was a living force and as such looked upon by all as worthy of reverent adhesion, the caste system was not unplastic or ossified and so gifted people, driven by an inner urge, were actually encouraged to change their vocation. An instance in point is King Viśvāmitra, who by arduous askesis rose from his native caste of Kṣatriya to that of a Brāhmin, an illuminate. Conversely, Droṇa, though born a Brāhmin, not only rose to fame as a mighty warrior but actually taught archery to the young princes, the sons of Pāṇḍu and Dhṛtarāṣṭra. The great Vidura, though the son of a Śūdra maid-servant, came to be revered as a holy man, so much so that he was hailed by King Dhṛtarāṣṭra as his monitor whose discourses on dharma and ethics were starred with jewelled sayings; and, last, though not least, he was ranked as one of the dearest friends of Kṛṣṇa himself; we witness — lo and behold ! — a veritable drama when the Blessed Lord turned away from the royal banquet of Duryodhana and went straight to the hut of poor Vidura to share his modest meal of *śākānna*, rice and vegetables, and passed the whole night, lying side by side with him on the same bed, discussing the things of the spirit.

I am not contending that the caste system as advocated by Kṛṣṇa in the Gita should continue today. That is to be decided ultimately by the pillars of society, the legislators and the illuminates who, with the light of their innate spiritual wisdom, can winnow away the chaff from the corn, initiating the reforms called for by the vanguard of the social conscience of today. This is all but certain, because the caste system which has prevailed uptill now is crumbling and even religious men are becoming more and more tolerant as the partition-walls are being whittled away. That 'the old order changeth yielding place to a new', is a fact which has been attested by history in all ages and climes. So I am not holding a brief for an intransigent caste system upheld by highbrow pedants and fanatical pundits who asseverate that what was good for our ancestors yesterday must be adjudged good for us today as well. Change is the law of life and a new age must engender a new Weltanschauung. The ideal of 'one world' has come to stay and do what we will we cannot possibly put back the hands of destiny's clock. One does, indeed, sometimes feel like regretting that, everything being mutable, a march forward should entail turning one's back on much that has materially helped one in the past — much that one would fain retain. But relentless time does often enough, like a flood, somewhat dim if not altogether obliterate the monuments, landmarks and prohibitions of the past, especially when it hurts, like shackles, our pilgrim feet aching to march onward. None on earth can have the argument both ways: hail the evolving joy of the new Advent and revive the receding traditions of the remote Past. Sri Aurobindo has written about this in an inspiring pronunciamento:

"We of the coming age stand at the head of a new age of development which must lead to a new and larger synthesis. We are not called upon to be orthodox Vedantins... or to adhere to one of the theistic religions of the past or to entrench ourselves within the four corners of the teachings of the Gita. That would be to limit ourselves and to attempt to create our spiritual life out of the being, knowledge and nature of others, of the men of the past instead of building it out of our own being and potentialities. We do not belong to the past dawns but to the noons of the future."[6]

No aspirant who has even a streak of the spiritual light in his soul can demur at this, the less so as no true seeker who thirsts for a divine fulfilment of mortality can wish to rest on his laurels. Sri Aurobindo stressed this years ago when he wrote to me :

"The traditions of the past are great in their own place. But that does not mean that we should go on repeating the past. A great tradition must be followed by a greater future."

So, if the protection our caste system gave to us all yesterday is found today to be inadequate — If, that is, we should find that we must build a new superstructure on our old stable plinth — we should not only not rue the necessity but gladly welcome His Flute-call today to a new Vṛndāvan where His triumphs of the past shall be supplemented by greater triumphs to be achieved by modern architects; and if they are master builders they will know how to use the material of our past experience to build a new synthesis in consonance with our svadharma today.

But it is of the first importance to know *how* we may achieve this in practice. For an ideal remains inoperative till it finds in the arena of life the means to realise the Goal it exhorts us to achieve. Sri Aurobindo has adumbrated the *modus operandi* at the end of the Chapter entitled "Our Demand and Need from the Gita":

"Our object, then, in studying the Gita," he writes, "will not be a scholastic or academical scrutiny of its thought, nor to place its philosophy in the history of metaphysical speculation, nor shall we deal with it in the manner of the analytical dialectician. *We approach it for help and light and our aim must be to distinguish its essential and living message, that in it on which humanity has to seize for its perfection and its highest spiritual welfare."* (emphasis mine).

I underline the last sentence not only to endorse whole-heartedly the wisdom of Sri Aurobindo's illumined vision, but also to profit by the hint he has given here to the effect that the Gita's teaching — if properly interpreted with all the light that has accrued to us from the messages of later messiahs — cannot but give us the much-needed "help and light" in our pilgrimage to the gleaming Goal of our mental, vital and psychic fulfilment.

The Gita's powerful and refreshing advocacy of the triune path of action, knowledge and devotion — *karma, jñāna* and *bhakti* — has helped countless seekers to evolve towards the light because the Gita sets store by the evolution of human nature from harmony to a higher harmony. A man may become a great artist and his art may delight us all, but we so often feel disappointed — or even shocked — when we miss in him the refreshing richness of a harmonious development of our physical, mental and spiritual powers. Art creates beauty and beauty ravishes the heart. But though "a thing of beauty is a joy for ever", because beauty manifests an aspect of divinity through the appeal of perfection of form, it can never give us a sense of complete fulfilment unless it conveys through beauty a thrilled touch of harmony. The poet Dryden was not wrong when he sang :

From harmony, from heavenly harmony
This universal frame began :
From harmony to harmony
Through all the compass of the notes it ran,
The diapason closing full in Man.

Man has been called the crown of creation because only he among God's creatures can satisfy the soul with an all-round harmonious development.

In *Aitareya Upaniṣad* there is a significant parable about the genesis of Man : God — *Atmā* — first created the gods (*devatāh*) who, falling into the trackless ocean of life, were subjected to hunger and thirst. But as they were still gods they wanted an earthly form through which they could appease their hunger and thirst and enjoy the cosmic play. So they appealed to the God of gods to provide them with an abode (*āyatanam*) which they could indwell so as to be able to thrive on a material pabulum. So God created first a cow for them. But as they found it unsatisfactory, He placed before them a horse which, too, they discarded as inadequate. The God, at long last, fashioned the human form which they acclaimed as harmonious (*sukṛtam*) and so consented to preside in him.

I exploit this time-old parable because it underlines the necessity of harmony and approves of it as creative of an atmosphere in which evolution can be promoted spontaneously. Shakespeare also enthused in Hamlet over man (though perhaps a little too ecstatically): "What a piece of work is a man ! how noble in reasons ! how infinite in faculty ! in form and moving how express and admirable ! in action how like an angel ! in apprehension how like a god !"

But alas, such an apotheosis of man evokes but the raised eyebrow and smile today. Why ? Because man has not justified the high hopes he inspired in the hearts of the gods and poets who hymned his glorious potentiality . I say 'potentiality' because when we look at the ravaged, blood-stained, war-torn arena of life, where men are massacred and millions consigned to slums and jails and concentration camps, we are not only reminded of Wordsworth's sigh: "What man has made of man!"—but cannot help but exclaim sadly with another idealist poet, Bret Harte:

Of all the words of tongue and pen
The saddest are — what might have been!

It is here that the Gita assures us (5.21) that "what might have been" can still be realised here and now provided we hark back to the Lord's clarion-call to tread the triune path of Yoga — knowledge, work and love which upleads the soul to the eternal union with God which is unending happiness — *sa Brahmayogayuktātamā sukham akṣayam aśnute* (5.21).

The realist-pessimist may carp at such a pronouncement contending that the askesis needed for such a fairy-tale consummation is and always shall gleam beyond the reach of poor earthlings who are too inextricably tethered to their suicidal impulses and dark cravings to dream of the heights which only the elect — the born mountaineers — can aspire to assault. So it is no good upbraiding them as the One on high did (*Sāvitri* 4.3):

O Force-compelled, Fate-driven earthborn race,
Petty adventurers in an infinite world
And prisoners of a dwarf humanity!
How long will you tread the circling tracks of mind
Around your little self and petty things?

But Kṛṣṇa does not stop at upbraiding: his message is essentially hortatory. That is why he assures Arjuna emphatically that what seems unreal to us on the planes of the lower consciousness can become here and now a rapturous reality if only we are vowed to climb to the plateaus of the higher consciousness on the wings of Yoga as outlined by Him.

But how are we to climb to the plateaus and Peak of Divine Consciousness? The answer is — by dint of persistent askesis and indomitable aspiration to be a mountaineer of Light through many lives. That is, being reborn time and again to resume climbing with a godly resolution to achieve the summit-vision of *Brāhmi sthiti* [7] — deep repose in the Divine consciousness.

The life that wins its aims asks greater aims,
The life that fails and dies must live again:
Till it has found itself it cannot cease. [8]

Kṛṣṇa gives Arjuna this guarantee — namely, that those who turn to Him wholeheartedly shall be guided by Him at every step (9.22) — and goes on to add that a man's evolution of consciousness cannot stop short at his death but spirals up sleeplessly through successive births till he attains to the pinnacle realisation that all is God, Vāsudeva.[9] As He repeated this momentous assertion in several couplets I may here pause for a little to refer in brief to His vision and pronouncement.

He says (2.27) that a man's rebirth after death is as certain as his death after birth and that this seemingly endless progression can come to an end only when the soul, after a cycle of successive births, attains to Him and abides there — which *is* the highest goal, the summam bonum of life (6.45).

In Hindu hagiography the reality of rebirth has been attested by great sages and saints as an incontrovertible fact. Not so in the occident.[10] The reason probably is that Christ never made any categoric pronouncement on the question but only assured all (who looked up to Him as God incarnate) that they could reach the final destination in Heaven where the Lord, the Father would give the heavy-laden spirits "the peace that passeth all understanding", provided they did *His* will, disowning their egoism and self-will. There is no hint at all about their rebirth in case they failed to do His will flawlessly. But the Gita takes its stand on a succession of births, every birth spurring the new-born aspirants ever onwards — or shall we say upward — towards the summit *Brahma nirvāṇa,* to achieve the final mergence in the Divine and reach a point of no return — *yaṁ prāpya na nivartante tad dhāma paramaṁ mama* (8.21).

Here the question asks itself — how could Kṛṣṇa hold forth this ideal of release from the cycle of birth and death ? To put it more explicitly, if the earth is to be regarded as an irredeemable house of sorrow and decay — *duḥkhālayam aśāśvatam* — (8.15) then why, in the name of mercy, did He send us to such a dismal planet? It is contended by some theologians that we have to be born again and again so that, having purified ourselves and realised our oneness with God, we may successfully conquer the downpull of birth and come home for ever. But such an escapist philosophy does not satisfy intellect and still less the soul which — after having realised His Grace through the triune Yoga of love, action and knowledge — finds that the earthlife despite its all-too-obvious limitations is assuredly not a dungeon of pain, but can be turned by our Yoga into an abode of song and beauty, art and science, light and joy culminating in a rapturous harmony, which Kṛṣṇa characterises as *samatā*, *Brāhmi sthiti* on the breath-taking playground of His utter Self, *Puruṣottama*. Sri Aurobindo has accepted this view and sung (Book XI, *Sāvitri*) :

Earth is the chosen place of mightiest souls,
Earth is the heroic spirits' battlefield,
The forge where the Arch-mason shapes His works.

But this marvellous truth cannot be realised till we attain the summit vision. At the present stage of human evolution we are hampered at every step by the God-hostile forces we harbour in ourselves. No wonder we miss the clue to His Light which pilots the soul to the heaven of His cosmic harmony, transforming hourly the elements which are at war with His divine Will. That is the reason why the *Avatāra* (Arch-mason) is born on earth from "age to age" as the Kindly Light to guide and train us all so we may change the thorns of our fallen nature into roses of our God-rapt Self.

But such a radical change cannot be encompassed overnight. We have to aspire for the Light, reject the lures which would draw us down and lastly, surrender our entire being to Him so that He may mould us to His Will thus "delivering us from all our sins"[11] and transforming us, things of repellent clay, into His "dear disciples,"[12] luminous and firm of tread. He comes to us as a World-Teacher, *Jagat-Guru,* because we, ignorant pilgrims, are constantly deceived, hailing flickering phantoms as the stellar reality. He is calling us all to follow His sungleam of vision and rejoice in His moonlight of Grace. We are slow to respond but the Blessed Lord is not one to accept defeat. He would not have created our earth and sought birth here time and again if He wanted to damn it finally as a "house of sorrow transient and dismal" (9.33). He comes to lead us on, compassionately, from a lower to a higher and richer harmony. Not for nothing did Sri Aurobindo reassure us in his beautiful epilogue to *Sāvitri* : "Heaven's touch fulfils but cancels not our earth."

Sri Aurobindo once wrote in a long poem entitled *The Life Heavens* extolling this unfolding harmony in the heart of struggling terrestrial nature : Mother Earth reveals to her son, Man, in a song:

O high seeker of Immortality
Is there not, ineffable, a bliss
Too vast for these finite harmonies
Too divine for the moment's unsure kiss.

I, Earth, have a deeper power than Heaven;
My lonely sorrow surpasses its rose-joys,
A red and bitter seed of the raptures seven;
My dumbness fills with echoes of a far Voice.

By me the last finite, yearning strives
To reach the last infinity's unknown.
The eternal is broken into fleeting lives
And Godhead pent in the mire and the stone.

I heckled him : how could he have seen in Earth what he had sung so ecstatically about — what was there so grand or glorious in Earth ? He answered in a letter :

"Where do you find in my *The Life Heavens* that the conditions on earth are glorious and suited to the Divine Life ? ...

The Earth is an evolutionary world.... most sorrowful, disharmonious, imperfect. Yet in that imperfection is the urge towards a higher and many-sided perfection. It contains 'the last finite' which yet yearns to be the supreme Infinite. God is pent in the mire (mire is not glorious so there is not claim to beauty or glory here) but that very fact imposes a necessity to break through the prison to a consciousness which is ever rising towards the heights... That is 'the deeper power' though not a greater actual glory or perfection."

In his *Sāvitri* (Book of Everlasting Day) he has vindicated Earth once again in a moved vision :

Heaven in its rapture dreams of the perfect earth,
Earth in its sorrow dreams of the perfect Heaven...
Since God made earth, earth must make in her God.

Yet the Gita refers now and again to the transient nature of the joys and excitements of the earth, but only to open Arjuna's eyes to the phantasmagoric aspect of a worldling's secular acclamation; for Kṛṣṇa, having the complete highest vision, has to admit that the pessimist-realist has indeed a case which is valid from his plane of lower earthly consciousness though not from that of the Divine Consciousness. In other words, He says in effect, one must not take the Appearance for the Reality — but learn to see things in the proper perspective. When one climbs a mountain along a path through a wood one cannot see what one visions athrill from the Peak — the glorious panorama of sky and clouds, light and shade, all cooperating to turn it into a rapturous experience (*Sāvitri*, 1.14):

A deathbound littleness is not all we are,
Immortal our forgotten vastnesses
Await discovery in our summit selves.

But the supreme discovery cannot be achieved without the sleepless propelling force of the Divine because only such a superhuman agency can deliver us from our blind attachment to sublunary pleasures, an attachment that seems to be ingrained in the very cells of our body. Or, to put it in the words of Sri Aurobindo (*Sāvitri*, 1.12) :

Only the Eternal's strength in us can dare
To attempt the immense adventure of the climb
And sacrifice of all we cherish here.

But though strength is a deep boon of His Grace, it cannot wean us from our cherished chains — nor can the mountaineer of aspiration climb to the pinnacle of Divine Love unless and until he cooperates with the Divine Grace, sworn once and for all to the pledge (*Sāvitri*, 3.2):

All that denies must be torn out and slain
And crushed the many longing for whose sake
We lose the one for whom our lives were made.

In Canto 15 Kṛṣṇa exhorts Arjuna to take the identical vow. He compares human life to a huge *Asvattha* tree, the cosmic tree of attachments whose branches impede all pilgrims of the stars. So, He enjoins Arjuna to be ruthless and says (15.3) that he must be determined to whittle away with the sword of non-attachment this firmly-rooted tree of craving and singing (15.4) :

I must first and foremost take refuge in the Primal Being,
Ādyam Puruṣaṁ.

Such a heroic feat needs strength which is available but only to those who have a burning aspiration to cut away from their moorings. This is by no means an easy task because our emotional self finds release from the sentimental cravings of the flesh a heartless if not cruel act. Rabindranath describes the anomalous nature of this pain very graphically with a simile :

Jarhāye āche bādhā chārhāye jete cai chārhāte gele byathā bāje.

That is :

My chains that hamper cling to me,
I long to cut them, but I'm pained to be rid of them.

We have seen how this pain made Arjuna cry out in an anguished outburst when he was exhorted to fight ruthlessly for truth and justice and how he protested in tears against Kṛṣṇa's clarion-call to chastise the wrongdoers. Kṛṣṇa chided him, saying that such a weak-kneed and lachrymose attitude was unworthy of him : he must follow his svadharma, repudiating the gospel of the coward who declines to act when action is incumbent on him.

Arjuna did love Kṛṣṇa with all his heart. But despite his adoration he vacillated, and so asked Kṛṣṇa whether one was doomed if on the path of Yoga one backslided. It is obvious from the context that Arjuna at this point was still somewhat diffident about himself and so wanted to be reassured that a stumble did not amount to a fall into the bottomless Pit. To this the Lord gave a memorable answer of compassion whose sweet cadence has instilled hope in the zero hour of despair of many an aspirant down the ages. He said in effect that a love which was essentially divine could not possibly consign a way-lost pilgrim to the Abyss because the Lord was the soul of forgiveness and mercy and came down to rehabilitate all who, on a sudden impulse, strayed away from the path. In the *Mahābhārata, Bhīṣmaparva,* too, there is a similar heart-warming assurance (given by Bhīṣma to Duryodhana) :

Ye tu Kṛṣṇaṁ prapadyante na te muhyanti mānavāḥ
Bhaye mahati magnan ca pāti nityaṁ Janārdanaḥ

Which means :

Who appeal to Kṛṣṇa never can fall, from deep
Catastrophies He'll save them every time.

In the *Bhāgavat* there is a still more emphatic reassurance :

svapādamulaṁ bhajataḥ priyasya
tvakvānyabhavasya Harih Pareśaḥ
vikarma yaccotpatitaṁ kathaṁ cit
dhunoti sarvaṁ hṛdi sanniviśṭaḥ

That is :

If you love the Lord one-pointedly and seek
Sincerely refuge at His lotus-feet,
Then even if you swerve from the path — He will,
Dwelling in the heart, absolve you from all sins.

In the Gita Kṛṣṇa delves a little deeper to allay Arjuna's fears. He says categorically (6.40) that one who is sincere can never come to grief because though man is prone to misunderstand God, God understands how weak man is, so, even when he falls accidentally, a chance is given again in his next birth. Not only that : because he stumbled on the path of sincere aspiration in his past birth he takes birth next time in the house of parents who are pure and prosperous. And even that is not the whole story, for he may be sent to be born in the family of yogis where the new-comer resumes his Yoga where he had left off in his previous birth (6.42-43). Kṛṣṇa Himself annotates His dictum that no sincere aspiration is lost — that is, what one has once realised in one's life can and does survive in the next. *En passant,* Rabindranath, too, stressed in a beautiful poem this reassuring spiritual truth in the divine scheme of life's ceaseless progression overriding all obstacles and interruption. He sang :

jibane jato pujā, holo na sārā
jāni he jāni tāo hai ni hārā
je phul nā phutite parheche dharanite
je nadi marupathe hārālo dhārā
jāni he jāni tāo hai ni hārā

That is :

I know : no single prayer of love, by life begun,
Though unsustained ;
No bud that ere it blossomed on the earth fell — wan
And shadow-stained ;
No ill-starred rill that pathless in the desert ran
Was lost, O Friend !

Egoistic efforts may bear no fruit on earth but no sincere aspiration is ever wasted — that is the heartening pronouncement of the Gita, so beautifully rendered by the poem just quoted. Such an asseveration is welcomed by the intellect because all waste of energy — especially when it is manifested through an idealistic aspiration — fills us with misgivings and prompts the mind to ask what is the point of it all. Is life only an eruption of arbitrary purposeless movements ? Is everything delightful but a brief and pointless dance of the nerves which will cease when the delights pall as they must ? Are we born unconsulted in a world only to be spirited away, unconsulted, in the end ? And must we revert finally to a Void of non-existence, a sheer gaping Nihil ? Is all beauty a make-believe, a sudden whim of a mysterious Being who just toys with things of beauty He creates in Nature — a whim which seems all the more cruel because of the hopes it inspires in the wistful heart ? If such be the case, then is it not crazy to sing hymns in a rapturous thanksgiving to a marvellous Creator who simply felt an unaccountable urge to make things only to smash it all into smithereens ? A religious poet, Rajanikanta, has posed this query in a moving song :

Anande ananta prān kariche bandanā gān
Abishrānta ananta nikhile :
Sakali ki arthahin shunya shunye habe leen
Tabe keno se giti srigile ?

That is :

Hark, the whole universe chants paeans to thee
In delight that knows no end,
And every heart is transformed into a shrine !
Can it be, alas, that all this ecstasy
Is vain ? Who then, O Friend,
Inspired us to compose such songs divine ?

Who puts the question ? Surely not the hard-boiled atheist who dismisses it all as a make-believe and answers with a wise smile : "If one is set on hoisting unwarrantedly a Creator as the initiator of His cosmic play, *Līlā,* one is welcome to his puerile enthusiasm, but I can plainly see that it is because you long to perpetuate your enjoyments that you posit an invisible Entity. Stay cushioned happily in your God-mooded illusions. Only bear in mind, please, that as no illusions can possibly survive the cruel blows of stark reality, you are likely to come to grief if you want to ride the rainbow. "A rational man," such a wise atheist will add sententiously, "should prefer to take life as he finds it and not lean on a foolish fancy, a coloured chimera..." and so on.

The answer has been given by the mystics in all ages : namely, that God seems a coloured chimera only to purblind materialist reason, not to the seer heart which can dive deep into the seemingly meaningless ocean of life and collect meaningful pearls of beauty and bliss created by Divine Grace :

Whose sweetness justifies life's blindest pain.[13]

Or, to put in the Gita's words (9.30-31) :

Even if a lost soul turns to me with a single-minded devotion, he shall soon win to the status of the saint and attain everlasting peace.

And Kṛṣṇa goes on to pledge His word to Arjuna (18.61-62) :

The Lord presides in the heart of all... seek refuge in Him in every way and you shall, by His Grace, reach the Eternal Abode of supreme Peace.

The long and short of it all is that the summit realisation of the One is not to be achieved on the plane of discursive reason of the sceptic who puts the questioning mind on the dais of the Chief Justice in whose dock the Lord when summoned has to stand to prove with humble arguments His mystic role as the Creator and Sustainer of the universe. The reason is simple, to wit, that though God can be experienced by the heart of devotion, He is too vast to be grasped or appraised by the ratiocinating intellect's sceptic yardstick or judicial galvanometer. The way to Him is paved first and last with aspiration for the Light, led by a spiritual intuition which accepts Him *a priori* but verifies it all subsequently by realising His Grace through an evolving love which, even when discouraged by the barren pain of no-experience, trusts in His promise that has resounded through the ages that He does answer our prayer (9.22):

Those who worship me focusing all their thoughts on me alone may rest assured that I shall procure them whatever they need and help them guard what they have garnered.

Lastly, He adds tenderly (9.26) :

Whoever offers me in simple love a leaf, a flower or even a drop of water, I accept in love.

Could the Divine give to us, flawed feckless creatures, a more touching testimony of His answering Grace than He did in the Gita in exquisite assurance such as these ?

Apropos, here is an unambiguous corroboration of what Sri Aurobindo once wrote to me : that Man would not have wanted the Divine if the Divine had not wanted Man. Years later he reaffirmed the obligation of this beautiful mutuality more fully (*Sāvitri,* 1.4):

He has made this tenement of flesh His own,
His image in the human measure cast,
That to His divine measure we might rise.
A mutual debt binds man to the Supreme :
His nature we must put on as He put ours ;
We are sons of God and must be even as He
His human portion, we must grow divine.

And that is why Sāvitri hails her heart's beloved as

My God is love and sweetly suffers all...
A traveller of the million roads of life (9.2).

Yes, that is surely one of the reasons why the Lord created the world of matter from star-dust, so that He might enjoy His cosmic play of transforming miraculously the tenacious terrestrial darkness into a divine illumination, wan matter into a resplendent receptacle of the soul, playing at hide and seek with His devotees on life's million roads. He, too, sang, in unison with Christ, that He sought birth on earth so He might, playing His rapturous game of Love's ever new sunrise, come to initiate a new human divine drama, *Nāralīlā,* with the sole object of flashing His sun-love of godly compassion in the antipodes of Light. In a word, Kṛṣṇa, like Christ, came to redeem His pledge to Earth that He would uplead our distracted planet to a harmonious Heaven, calling Himself unequivocally both as (7.9): "*puṇyo gandhaḥ pṛthivyāṁ ca tejaś cā 'smi vibhāvasau* : I am at once the sacred scent of the earth and the radiant energy of the fire." He ordained that men should be born again and again to evolve from the denial of darkness towards the affirmation of dawn, to march from the unreal to the Real, to rise from the death of hope to rapturous realisation. Now and again He refers, indeed, to the minor gods but not to encourage the elect to worship them for boons or favours (even though He does not frown on such suppliants, for He says in effect (7.21) that those who are not evolved enough to seek Him may worship these lesser gods with His temporary sanction) but to stress that He sheds His Grace only on those who turn to Him. Explaining it more emphatically, He adds (7.23) that those who turn to the lesser gods win only transient boons whereas those who turn to Him come straight to Him, the ultimate Divine. Could there be any reassurance of fulfilment more enthralling than this ?

Nowadays one is often told that the cult of personality is wholly wrong in that it encourages hero-worship. But the emotion which leads the heart to worship great personalities or heroes is one of the greatest boons that the Divine in His Grace has conferred on man in that it delivers the worshipper out of the prison of the ego with a radiant joy that is too spontaneous and satisfying to be questioned. How often have we not wished to be able to fly unimpeded in the sky outsoaring the dark dungeon of our stifling ego ! Stifling because it is so barren. Kṛṣṇa tells us time and again that only when you offer your heart to the Lord of your heart or emulate the great can you feel truly freed from the ego's cage against whose bars your bird-soul beats its bleeding wings.

The reason is that only when one follows an urge to worship the highest or feel a kinship with the saints and sages who have broken their cages' iron bars can one learn to experience the peace of blue freedom — *nirvāṇa* beyond the pale of earth's miasmas and glooms (6.15). For only then can one feel that one has at long last overpassed the vales of tormenting desires and lonely sorrows and achieved Godlove and good-will to all earthlings through the miracle power of love. And what happens then ? — One comes to experience vividly in his soul the quintessence of divinity and gain the supreme vision of His true Self — One and multitudinous[14] — thus winning the passport to the holy of holies (18.55). True, this marvellous vision can be had through the worship of the Impersonal and Unmanifest as well, but the profound bliss and peace that permeate your soul when you know Him intimately as the supreme Personality, *Puruṣottama,* can be attained only by the great Vision of His ineffable Grace which descends into you as spontaneously as the sunlight descends on earth at daybreak.

Personality cult ! One marvels when reading history how the course of things has been changed from time to time by a single personality who may well claim, in the words of Sri Aurobindo : "He made of the miracle a normal act !" How by their impact have a Kṛṣṇa, a Buddha, a Christ, an Ashok, a St. Francis, a Martin Luther, an Abraham Lincoln and ever so many creative personalities left a deep dent on the trend of the time ! A thoughtful writer has written, very cogently, that if a dozen great men of science were not born the peak of human achievements would not today be stared at in amazement by the common man, nor the life of day by day changed beyond recognition. Kṛṣṇa is, indeed, a breathtaking instance of one man bringing off a veritable revolution not only in the outer life of His contemporaries but in the basic outlook of Arjuna, his chief representative and flame-child of the age. And how He acted ! Not as a declared warrior outgeneraling the wicked foes' chief leaders but as a supreme strategist and dynamic champion of dharma against iniquity, strength against sentimentality, tranquil wisdom against vaunting folly, gold of sunshine against the mists of inertia !

I have divagated a little but only to suggest that Kṛṣṇa was not merely an evangelist of a gospel which reconciled the irreconcilable strands of the human aspirant but a tremendous man of action as well, whose divine gleam had to abolish the demon darkness of blatant usurpers to inaugurate a new era of light, to establish a *dharma-rājya*, like the proverbial phoenix out of the ashes of the dead past. This is not a mere picturesque metaphor. For if one reads between the lines of the Gita one cannot help but see that Arjuna as a generalissimo had all but succumbed and so had to be resurrected by the galvanizing war-conch of the divine Sponsor of a new harmony in which the eternally weak and discordant elements in man had to be woven into a noble synthesis welding together an evolved man's three major aspirations : knowledge, action and love. India has been a land of mighty personalities. But has there ever been such a many-mooded and colossal personality like Kṛṣṇa in whom multiple forces coalesced into a harmonious whole ? A romantic swain, a loving comrade, a loyal friend, a lovely lover, a radiant king, an inspiring philosopher, a divine legislator, a consummate artist, a marvellous minister, a dexterous charioteer, a Guru of gurus — above all, a messiah of incomparable wisdom whose message left an indelible stamp not only on the minds of his contemporaries but on the world-view of a grateful and enriched posterity. For it was His dictum that every impulse, action and thought offered to God in the right spirit must lead to liberation (summed up in Canto 9.27)[15] that inspired throughout the ages countless aspirants who looked up to Him for His lead of light. Not only that : this memorable couplet electrified the great Tantric illuminates who hailed earth as the sacred arena to plant the seed of dedicated action and made them improvise on the Gita's dictum in another memorable couplet which they accepted as their mantra of Yoga (*Mahānirvāṇa Tantra*) :

Prātarutthāya sāyāhnāt sāyāhnāt prātarantataḥ
Yat karomi Jaganmātas — tadeva tava pūjnaṁ

That is :

From sunrise to next sunrise whatever I do
Is an offering, Mother, of worship at thy feet !

In the Gita Kṛṣṇa adumbrated His mystic philosophy in a very simple way. He took, one by one, mainly three strands or themes: the Yoga of action, the Yoga of knowledge and the Yoga of devotion or God-love. It is essentially a synthesis which He wanted to commend to Arjuna for acceptance, but repeating intermittently : "Awake, arise, my friend, accept the challenge of life and face up to what you have got to do, following your svadharma — never be a day-dreamer, a lotus-eater, still less a coward escapist — *sarveṣu kāleṣu mām anusmara yudhya ca* — go on fighting for truth and justice all the time remembering me." (8.7)

But one can hardly stress any single tenet of a high philosophy or mystic gospel without, for a time, leaving unstressed its other findings. So, although in Kṛṣṇa's comprehensive message even the seemingly contradictory elements do fall into place harmoniously like a jig-saw puzzle, He had to convey it all in an analytic vein and so could not obviate the limitations inherent in the approach of the analytic intellect. One of these is that one has to dissect one at a time what it examines or explains and so has to focus all the available light on just one strand of the philosophy excluding, for the nonce, the other strands. One result of such a procedure is that the light on the other strands gets temporarily somewhat dimmed, but unfortunately, it cannot be helped since, I repeat, whenever one concentrates on any one aspect of an exposition one is compelled, for a time, to shove aside the other aspects. That is one of the reasons why a partisan exegete could flourish this or that selected couplet of the Gita as Kṛṣṇa's cardinal pronouncement — now on love, now on knowledge, now on action. But if one appraises the Gita with a tranquil and impartial eye, one cannot possibly miss this all-too-patent fact that Kṛṣṇa described the excellence of one thread after another only to weave them together, ultimately, into a lovely quilt of harmony in an utterly disharmonious and distracted world. So now He says (4.37-38) : "The fire of knowledge reduces to cinder all action and there is nothing on earth as pure as the Yoga of knowledge," and then, lo, goes on to proclaim (11.54) :

"Only one-pointed devotion can know, see and enter into the quintessence of my Being" and lastly, assures us (18.46) : "A man can fully realise the Goal of self-fulfilment by propitiating with his action the One who pervades the world and is the fount and source of the cosmic urge to ceaseless action."

In one of his most impressive dissertations in the Gita Kṛṣṇa gives lucid and comprehensive illustrations of how the three essential modes of energy, the gunas, act in and through life : *sattva, rajas* and *tamas.* As He is at great pains to describe how these three modes make themselves felt in the different spheres of our life and self-expression (e.g, food, benefactions, faith, sacrifice, joy, askesis... et cetera) I cannot in trying to explain the gradations do better than quote *in toto* Sri Aurobindo's luminous exegesis in his *Essays on the Gita* (Chapter VI, First Series) :

> *Man meets the battle of life in the manner most consonant with the essential quality most dominant in his nature. There are, according to the Sāṁkhya philosophy accepted in this respect by the Gita, three essential qualities or modes of the world-energy and therefore also of human nature, sattva, the mode of poise, knowledge and satisfaction, rajas, the mode of passion, action and struggling emotion, tamas, the mode of ignorance and inertia. Dominated by tamas, man does not so much meet the rush and shock of the world energies whirling about him and converging upon him as he succumbs to them, is overborne by them, afflicted, subjected; or at the most, helped by the other qualities, the tāmasik man seeks only somehow to survive, to subsist as long as he may, to shelter himself in the fortress of an established routine of thought and action in which he feels himself to a certain extent protected from the battle, able to reject the demand which his higher nature makes upon him, excused from accepting the necessity of farther struggle and the ideal of an increasing effort and mastery. Dominated by rajas, man flings himself into the battle and attempts to use the struggle of forces for his own egoistic benefit, to slay, conquer, dominate, enjoy; or, helped by a certain measure of the sāttvik quality the rājasik man makes the struggle itself a means of increasing inner mastery, joy, power, possession. The battle of life becomes his delight and passion partly for its own sake, for the pleasure of activity and the sense of power, partly as a means of his increase and natural self-development. Dominated by sāttvik, man seeks in the midst of strife for a principle of law, right, poise, harmony, peace, satisfaction. The*

purely sāttvik man tends to seek this within, whether for himself alone or with an impulse to communicate it, when won, to other human minds but usually by a sort of inner detachment from or else an outer rejection of the strife and turmoil of the active world-energy; but if the sāttvik mind accepts partly the rājasik impulse, it seeks to impose this poise and harmony upon the struggle and apparent chaos, to vindicate a victory for peace, love and harmony over the principle of war, discord and struggle. All the attitudes adopted by the human mind towards the problem of life derive from the domination of one or other of these qualities or else from an attempt at balance and harmony between them.

As Sri Aurobindo has beautifully explained how the three modes act in life — which hardly needs any further commentary, I will confine myself to elucidating only one point that has not been annotated in the excerpt quoted. It is about three kinds of happiness men feel in life ; *sāttvik, rājasik* and *tāmasik.* Kṛṣṇa says that all endeavours that taste in the beginning like poison and in the end like nectar are to be regarded as *sāttvik* (18.37); those that are delightful at the beginning but end in deep distaste, like poison, are *rājasik* by nature (18.38) and those pleasures which start with a kind of delusion, *moha* and end also in delusion or stem from somnolence, indolence or negligence are essentially *tāmasik* in character (18.39). These are very important definitions, the more so as a spiritual aspirant has to decide almost at every step which path to choose and which to reject.

When, however, one has ventured to describe however briefly the action of the triple gunas, one is, willy-nilly, confronted with the exceedingly difficult question of the state of consciousness which the Gita calls *triguṇātīta* or *nistraiguṇya.*

Fortunately for us, Sri Aurobindo has tackled the question brilliantly in his *Essays on the Gita* in the chapter entitled, "Beyond the Gunas." As I cannot add anything more cogent to his masterly exposition I will confine myself to quoting what the great Śaṁkarācārya has said in his masterpiece *Viveka Cūḍāmaṇi* by way of commentary to Kṛṣṇa's exhortation to transcend the gunas in the oft-quoted couplet (2.45) :

Traiguṇyaviṣayā vedā nistraiguṇyo bhavār' juna !
Nirdvandvo nityasattvastho niryogakṣema ātmāvan

Which means :

> *The way the three gunas act in life is the theme of the Vedas, but you, Arjuna, must transcend them, poised in the divine consciousness beyond the dualities and modes and, reposing utterly in your inmost soul, you must abolish once and for all the restlessness that dogs us all when we desire anything or long to retain what we desire.*

Śaṁkarācārya explains the three gunas :

Sattva guṇa is pellucid like the pure water. But commingling with *rajas* and *tamas* it leads to bondage. For all that, when it reflects the beneficent light of the soul it reveals, like the sun, the entire world (117).

Rajas is the spring of action and constitutes the primal urge of the earthling to take part in the life of desire and as such is responsible for all the deviations of the mind entailing the dark brood of pain and frustration (111).

And what is *tamas* ? He equates it with all the proclivities and moods which harbour ignorance, petrifaction, somnolence and folly and adds that when caught in this unhappy snare (of *tamas*) the dullard can understand nothing and only bears witness to things like an inanimate pillar (116).

But in life, as the Gita says, none of these three gunas can help but coexist together, so that even *sattva* has to admit *rajas* and *tamas* under its aegis. Therefore, adds Kṛṣṇa the only way out is to rise above even the *sattva* to emerge into the inviolate light of liberation of *śuddha-sattva*[16] which Śaṁkarācārya defines thus beautifully in his *Viveka Cūḍāmaṇi* (119):

> *Viśuddha-sattvasya guṇāh prasādaḥ svātmānubhūtiḥ paramā praśāntiḥ*
> *Triptiḥ praharṣaḥ paramātmaniṣṭhā yayā sadānandarasam samricchati*

Which means that this mode beyond the triple gunas — to wit, *viśuddha-sattva* — boons one with a deep felicity, self-realisation, profound peace, sense of fulfilment, delight and an unswerving devotion to the Supreme which showers the aspirant with an unwarning bliss.

Eminent commentator and savant Dvijendranath Tagore prefers to substitute, a la Śaṁkarācārya, the word *śuddh-asattva* for *triguṇātīta*. So I too may safely follow in his footstep.

He has explained it all with a wealth of cogent and apposite images which are all but impossible to translate without doing him a grave injustice. Nevertheless I cannot resist the temptation of translating the exquisite opening lines of his *Gita-path* as a parenthesis, the less so as it is one of the finest tributes I have ever read to the deathless message of the Song of songs, the Gita. He begins thus straightaway :

> *This is Santiniketan. In my little hut a perennial lamp is still burning without oil ; the lamp of the Bhagavad Gita. Storm after storm have swept over our country but glory to the Lord — the flickerless effulgence of this lamp has never once dimmed — but goes on shedding its lovely lustre everlastingly. The sum total light of all the cumulative radiance of Western mysticism — the radiance that has for long suffused the sky from end to end — has not been able to outvie the indomitable flame of our little lamp which lifts its marvellous head above all other lanterns. It emits a kind of subtle vapour which purifies the atmosphere of our country and the snow-white cloud-land of this holy vapour showers water-drops of a peace which soothes and revives our care-worn hearts like rejuvenating nectar—nay, it builds a veritable stairway to Immortality.*

Now to resume my thread and sum up : one has to remember that this *triguṇātīta* state can be attained by dint of Yoga and that it is free from the limitations of even the *sattva guna* (not to mention *rajas* and *tamas*) and as such must be hailed as the highest status a spiritual aspirant can aspire to in his cosmic pilgrimage.

But through man-made definitions one cannot elucidate what it actually is in essence, how it presides and endows man with the immaculate consciousness, thus enabling him not only to achieve liberation from all bondage — outsoaring the din and mists of terrestrial life — but vouchsafes to him the summit vision which alone can give him the highest fulfilment on the Gita's triune path of action, knowledge and love (*karma, jñāna* and *bhakti*).

But this highest fulfilment cannot be attained so long as one stays (in Sri Aurobindo's words) "enslaved by the gunas, now hampered in the dull ease of *tamas*, now blown by the strong winds of *rajas*, now limited by the partial lights of *sattva*... He is therefore mastered by pain and pleasure, happiness and grief, desire and passion, attachment and disgust."

That is why it is incumbent on the spiritual aspirant to outsoar the valley of the gunas in order to rest on the peak of the *śuddha-sattva*. And this can be done (as Sri Aurobindo avers) only when one aspires sleeplessly to the Gita's *Puruṣottama* superconsciousness, as I have already mentioned elsewhere in another excerpt from Sri Aurobindo's *Essays on the Gita*. Those who want to know more are referred to his comprehensive exposition and the luminous discourses of Dvijendranath. So I will conclude this section with a revealing parable of the great messiah Ramakrishna, the more so as it makes the function of the gunas and the *triguṇātīta* consciousness a little more understandable to the human mind, straining ceaselessly to grasp with the mind a Realisation beyond the ambit of the intellect :

A man, pathlost in a deep forest, was waylaid by three robbers A, B and C. The robber A, after despoiling the wayfarer of all he had, bound him hand and foot and said : "Now let us go." The robber B said : "No, have pity on the poor fellow. We have robbed him of everything he had. Why add insult to injury by pinioning him ? Let us set him free" — and so he unstrapped him. The third robber, C wanting to be more helpful, took him in tow and led him to the edge of the forest where he paused and said : "My good friend, the utmost I can do for you now is to show you the way out of the forest and indicate the road ahead that leads to the village. Look, there is the road : I wish you godspeed."

So you see, A, that is, tamas, wanted to reduce the captive into an immobile object. The second, B — standing for rajas — had commiseration, being more evolved, and so persuaded his friends to set him free. The third robber, C (sattva), being still more evolved, wanted to help him by showing him the way out of the dense forest. But even he — being a robber, in the last analysis could not venture to escort him back to the village.

Commentary on the revealing parable is superfluous. The long and short of it is that in order to arrive one must steadily follow the upward slope of evolution, from *tamas* to *rajas*, and then from *rajas* to *sattva*. But even *sattva* must be transcended if one thirsts for the highest Light and Beatitude.

I may here pause for a little to explain at some length the difficulty about high mystic terminology. The poet A.E. once wrote to me in a letter (dated 6.1.1932) :

> *English is a great language but it has very few words relating to spiritual ideas. For example, the word karma in Sanskrit embodies a philosophy. There is no word in English embodying the same idea. There are many words in Sanskrit charged with meanings which have no counterpart in English — words like dhyāni, suṣupti, turīya et cetera — and I am sure the language the Hindus speak today must be richer in words fitting for spiritual expression than English, in which there are few luminous words that can be used when there is a spiritual emotion to be expressed.*

Sri Aurobindo also must have experienced the same difficulty when translating words in the Gita — like svadharma, *svabhāva, tapas,* gunas, *puruṣa* — even as I myself was held up similarly many a time till a happy device occurred to me — to put in my translations of Sanskrit metres into English blank verse the Sanskrit words in apposition as, for example :

> *Gunas or modes of Nature, Prakṛti — five feet iambic. (14.5)*
> *But tamas (inertia) stems from ignorance — five feet iambic. (14.8)*
> *Abandoning all codes of conduct (dharma) — five feet iambic. (18.66)*

But I was in deep waters when I was called upon to translate *tapas* or *tapasyā*. A few translators have rendered it sometimes by austerities sometimes by penance. But I found both these words unsatisfactory. Nor would meditation or concentration be adequate. In his *Essays on the Gita,* Sri Aurobindo has translated it by the Greek word *askesis.* But I hesitated till I found in the Oxford Dictionary, Volume XIII, askesis accepted. Here is what is written :

> *Ascesis also askesis — practice of self-discipline. 1880 Pater Greek Studies (1904) 254. The sanity of soul and body... the perfecting of both by reasonable exercise or ascesis. 1890 E. Johnson Rise Christendom 107. In the conduct of life they establish a strict ascesis... as a means of closer communion with the Divine.*

Thereafter I have made use of this felicitous word freely even as I have used a few other Sanskrit words — like dharma, mantra, sadhu, Om — that is, words which have been stamped as current coin in English.

I may mention here that I have rendered *trance* by the word *samādhi* as it, too, has been accepted as an English word. The Oxford Dictionary, Volume XIII, gives :

> *Samādhi — Profound or abstract meditation on the Supreme Being; the last stage of Yoga, in which it is held that there is a suspension of connection between soul and body.*

The word *Guṇa* has also been made welcome. The Oxford Dictionary, Volume XIII, writes :

> *Guṇa — In the Sāṁkhya philosophy of India any one of the three principles of nature.*

One of the most important words of which there is no English equivalent is the word *dharma*. Oxford Dictionary has fortunately accepted this word, only the Gita uses the word in a far more comprehensive sense. The dictionary explains thus:

> *Dharma — Right behaviour, virtue, righteousness, in Buddhism, the law.*

But, as Sri Aurobindo has stressed, this word in Hindu mysticism has a world of deep and varied implications. He writes in his *Essays on the Gita*, First Series, Chapter XVII:

> *Dharma in the Indian conception is not merely the good, the right, morality and justice, ethics; it is the whole government of all the relations of man with other beings, with Nature, with God, considered from the point of view of a divine principle working itself out in forms and laws of action, forms of the inner and the outer life, orderings of relations of every kind in the world. Dharma (the word means "holding" from the root dhṛ, to hold) is both that which we hold to and that which holds together our inner and outer activities. In its primary sense it means a fundamental law of our nature which secretly conditions all our activities, and in this sense each being, type, species, individual, group has its own dharma. Secondly, there is the divine nature which has to develop and manifest in us, and in this sense dharma is the law of the inner workings by which that grows in our being. Thirdly, there is the law by which we govern our outgoing thought and action and our relations with each other so as to help best both our own growth and that of the human race towards the divine ideal.*

It is in this sense that the seer-poet Vyāsa extolled dharma in the last Canto of the last book of the *Mahābhārata :*

Na jātu kāmān na bhayān na lobhāt
Dharmaṁ tyajet jeevitasyāpi hetoḥ
Nityo dharmaḥ *sukha duḥkhe tvanitye*
Jeevo nityo heturasya tvanityaḥ

That is:

Thou shalt not disown dharma on earth, impelled
By lust, fear or cupidity, for know
That dharma is eternal, whereas joy
And pain are transient : the soul is everliving,
Although its basis in the world's unstable.

Now I will conclude with what I feel to be the most inspiring message of the Gita : namely that of *bhakti* — devotion, love divine. *Apropos,* I am reminded of a moving poem of Shelley in which he interprets love as worship — dedication of the heart's devotion. It has been hailed by Sri Aurobindo as one of Shelley's most psychic poems :

I can give not what men call love
But wilt thou accept not
The worship the heart lifts above
And the heavens reject not :
The desire of the moth for the star,
Of the night for the morrow,
The devotion to something afar
From the sphere of our sorrow ?

Commenting on this poem Sri Aurobindo wrote to me nearly forty years ago:

Shelley says in substance : "Human vital love is a poor inferior thing, a counterfeit of true love, which I cannot offer to you. But there is a greater thing, a true psychic love, all worship and devotion, which men do not really value, being led away by the vital glamour, but which the Heavens do not reject though it is offered from something far below them, so maimed and ignorant and sorrow-vexed as the human consciousness which is to the divine consciousness as the moth is to the star, the night to day. And will you not accept this from me, you, who in your nature are kin to the Heavens, you, who seem to me to have something of the divine nature, to be something bright and happy and pure far above the 'sphere of our sorrow ?' "

(I must mention, in parenthesis, that Sri Aurobindo uses the adjective 'psychic' in a sense different from the common acceptation of the term. In all his writings he has implied by psychic love an offering of the soul as against the claims of the vital love out to desire, possess and enjoy through power or sensual gratification).

Kṛṣṇa in the Gita and the *Bhāgavat* means this psychic love whenever he extols *bhakti*, insisting all the time that authentic *bhakti* though it includes a psychic emotion does not stop there but is on wings to offer all one has to the Beloved in unquestioning and total self-surrender.

Sri Aurobindo writes in his *Synthesis of Yoga*, (Part 3, Chapter 1):

Love is the crown of all being and its way of fulfilment, that by which it rises to all intensity and all fullness and the ecstasy of utter self-finding... Love is the power and passion of the divine self-delight and without love we may get the rapt peace of its infinity or the absorbed silence of the ānanda, but not its absolute depth or richness and fullness.

And he goes on to add :

Love fulfilled does not exclude knowledge, but itself brings knowledge; and the completer the knowledge, the richer the possibility of love. "By Bhakti", says the Lord in the Gita, "shall a man know me in all my extent and greatness and as I am in the principles of my being, and, when he has known Me in the principles of my being, then he enters into me." (11.54)

Kṛṣṇa reverts again and again to *bhakti* in different contexts and everytime He does so He stresses the psychic (*sāttvik*) element in it as against the vital (*rājasik*). For instance, when He speaks to Arjuna about the devotees who are dear to Him, He says (7.17) :

Among the various illuminates those who love me one-pointedly are closest to my heart even as I am closest to them.

And He says in the next Canto (8.22):

The Supreme in whom dwell all sentient creatures, and who pervades the universe can be realised only by single-minded devotion.

Kṛṣṇa is not opposed to rituals when these are supported by the psychic (*sāttvik*) love (9.13-14) :

The illuminates whose natures are receptive to my divinity and who hail me as the Primal Parent of all that is, turn to worship me with an unfaltering love, bow to me in adoration and sing my Name day after blissful day.

In India millions of His devotees turn to Him either singing His holy Name day after resonant day or repeating it as a mantra on their hearts' rosaries. Among these there are the blessed illuminates whom Kṛṣṇa cherishes tenderly because their knowledge derives from their mystic devotion (10.8-9-10) :

The illuminates who know that I am the Primal Origin of all adore me as such in love's deep ecstasy, focusing their minds and hearts on me. And they dwell in unutterable joy on this one blessed theme day after rapturous day, delighting one another. To such dedicated souls who live to love me sleeplessly, rapt in me, I grant the mind of light so they may attain to me.[17]

To quote now three closing couplets at the end of Canto 11, if only to underline how the Lord stresses the supremacy of love and what He means by Love. He says to Arjuna :

What I have revealed to you cannot be achieved through a mastery of hoary scriptures, askesis, benefactions or sacrifices. Only by dint of a world-oblivious love can you know and see and enter into the core of my Being. And lastly, let me emphasise that the devotee who offers all his works to me, who is dedicated to me, delivered from all attachments and who bears ill-will to none comes home to me. (11.53-54-55)

One of the reasons why Kṛṣṇa had to underline the mystic power of love to pilot the frail bark of that half despondent boatman, the human seeker, is that the Upaniṣads which were regarded as the highest and stablest basis of spiritual askesis passed by *bhakti* as the cult of the weak who were not eligible for the highest Realisation *nirvikalpa samādhi*. Only in *Svetāśvatara Upaniṣad* occurs the word *bhakti* and that also once, in the last couplet (6.23):

Yasya deve parā bhaktir-yathā deve tathā Gurau
Tasyaite kathitā hyarthāh prakāshante mahātmanaḥ

That is :

The inmost meaning of this lore of Light
Is revealed but to the great illuminates
Who cherish the Guru and God with devotion.

I am not suggesting that the Upaniṣads actually looked down on devotion. Whosoever will touch God is bound to be thrilled with love that His touch inspires. But this much is certain, that the Vedic seers and sages sought primarily the key of knowledge, *jñāna* and not that of Godlove, *bhakti*, when they aspired to open the lock of His starry treasury. That is why, in the Gita, Kṛṣṇa emphasized time and again the supreme power of Godlove to boon us with angel wings to take us to the Zenith Realisation. Nay, He said repeatedly, with all the emphasis His panegyrics of love could command, that devotion, *bhakti*, is not only not redundant in the Yoga of the triune path but can fill the long deserts on the way to Him with fragrance and music, peace and beauty and above all, with radiant signs of His proximity. Sri Aurobindo too endorsed this interpretation in his masterly exegesis. In the last chapter of his *Essays on the Gītā* (entitled, Message of the Gita) :

An entire Godlove, and adoration extends to a love, of the world and all its forms and powers and creatures in all the Divine is seen, is found, is adored, is served or is felt in oneness. Add to knowledge and works this crown of the eternal triune delight, admit this love, learn this worship : make it one spirit with works and knowledge. That is the apex of the perfect perfection.

This Yoga of love will give you a highest potential force for spiritual largeness and unity and freedom. But it must be a love which is one with God-knowledge. There is a devotion which seeks God in suffering for consolation, succour and deliverance : there is a devotion which seeks Him for His gifts, for divine aid and protection and as a fountain of the satisfaction of desire ; there is a devotion that, still ignorant, turns to Him for light and knowledge... But when the God-lover is also the God-knower, the lover becomes oneself with the Beloved... Develop in yourself this God-engrossed love; the heart spiritualised and lifted beyond the limitations of its lower nature will reveal to you most intimately the secrets of God's immeasurable being, bring into you the whole touch and influx and glory of His divine powers and open to you the mysteries of an eternal rapture....

This love that is knowledge, this love that can be the deep heart of your action, will be your most effective force for an utter consecration and complete perfection. An integral union of the individual's being with the Divine Being is the condition of a perfect spiritual life. Turn then altogether towards the Divine; make one with Him by knowledge, love and works all your nature. Turn utterly towards Him and give up ungrudgingly into His hands your mind and your heart and your will, all your consciousness and even your very senses and body. Let your consciousness be sovereignly moulded by Him into a flawless mould of His divine consciousness. Let your heart become a lucid or flaming heart of the Divine. Let your will be an impeccable action of His will. Let your very sense and body be the rapturous sensation and body of the Divine. Adore and sacrifice to Him with all you are; remember Him in every thought and feeling, every impulsion and act. Persevere until all these things are wholly His and He has taken up even in most common and outward things as in the inmost sacred chamber of your spirit his constant transmuting presence.

Notes

1 It must be noted here that the word *svadharma* cannot be adequately translated by *duty* which is imposed by man's social conscience. I have myself made use of this word in my English translation because there is no other word available. So I must remind the reader that *svadharma* is essentially the line of conduct prescribed by our inner nature or psychic being whereas duty is sponsored primarily by the mind.

2 *Tasya bhasa sarvam idaṁ vibhati* (*Kaṭha Upaniṣad*, 2.2.15).

3 *Yogināḥ karma kurvanti saṅgaṁ tvaktvā 'tmaśuddhaye* (5.11). Yogis do everything with non- attachment to purify themselves from all that binds.

4 The reference is to *Kaṭha Upaniṣad's* pregnant satire about a blind man presuming to guide those who have no vision: *andhenaiva niyamana yathāndha* (1.2.5).

5 Message of the Gita (last chapter of *Essays on the Gita*).

6 Chapter 1, *Essays on the Gita.*

7 The *Brāhmi sthiti* or poise divine, says the Gita, delivers one from all illusion and leads him into the heart of bliss sustained by the divine consciousness (2.72).

8 *Sāvitri* (2.6).

9 The Gita (7.19). *Vāsudevaḥ sarvamiti sa mahātmā sudurlabhaḥ.*

10 Though the Psychic Research Society in the West has compiled a mass of evidence coming from departed spirits in support of the cosmic reality of rebirth, no Western mystic of repute regards rebirth as anything but a speculation.

11 *Ahaṁ tvā sarvapāpebhyo mokṣayiṣyāmi* (The Gita, 18.66).

12 *Priyo'si me* (18.65).

13 *Sāvitri*, The Book of Everlasting Day.

14 In every heart is hidden the myriad One—*Sāvitri*, (9.2).

15 *Yat karoṣi yad aśnāsi yaj-juhośi dadāsi yat*
Yat tapasyasi kaunteya ! tat kuruṣva madarpaṇam (9.27).
Which means:
Whatever you do, enjoy or sacrifice — whatever you give away to others, whatever askesis you undertake to attain my Grace — all you must offer to me, first and last.

16 Śaṁkarācārya here calls the *triguṇātīta* state — (the Gita's *nityā-śuddha*) —*viśuddha-sattva* alias *śuddha-sattva.*

17 Sri Ramana Maharṣi, one of the greatest yogis of this century, told me that he regarded *bhakti* as *jñāna-mātā*, that is, love is the mother of knowledge.

The Gita for Modern Man

Krishna Chaitanya

The essential message of the Gita is that if man does not study the deep structure of the world-system and derive his imperatives from it, the world will collapse around him and bury him in its ruins. This study brings out the vibrant contemporaneity of the message of the Gita, its redemptive promise in the modern world menaced by extinction.

"A profoundly important book, every page of which is permeated with an integrative energy that welds in lucid prose, insights, ideas and facts drawn from an astonishing range of disciplines."

The Book Review

"If a book can save the world, here it is."

Amrita Bazar Patrika

"Perhaps no recent commentator has done the Gita as much justice, in the light of what today we know of the world and ourselves, as this one."

India International Quarterly

ISBN 81-85120-27-7 22 x 28 cms 256 pages
5 colour, 14 b/w plates 3rd edn Rs. 375

The Betrayal of Krishna

VICISSITUDES OF A GREAT MYTH

Krishna Chaitanya

Hailed as Indian approximation to the Renaissance man, Krishna Chaitanya has, to his credit many multi-volume works on philosophy, literature and arts. A continuation of his concerns of his earlier books on the Mahabharata and the Gita, here he clarifies the implications of the entire spectrum of rich meanings to which the Krishna myth is escalated in the epic and its great inset dialogue, details their loss through distortion by schoolman philosophy and incursion of literary dilettantism and erotic romanticism and brings out the vibrant contemporary relevance of the great myth for the redemption of modern man.

"A fabulous encyclopaedia of Hindu philosophy, modern science and anguished ego consciousness. The positive and affirmative philosophy of both personal and social virtue is insisted upon throughout the book. Krishna Chaitanya has almost completely exhausted the possibilities of research on the Krishna myth."

The Hindustan Times

ISBN 81-85120-39-0

14 x 22 cms   560 pages   Rs.360

Mysticism

Sisirkumar Ghose

The imbalance of our civilization, so much know-how and so little know-why has no other cure than a balanced mysticism. Presented in this volume are 45 essays by one of the sharpest thinkers of our time.

National Fellow (1974-76) and National Lecturer (1982-83), Sisirkumar Ghose has numerous publications to his credit, including *The Later Poems of Tagore, The Poetry of Sri Aurobindo, Meta-Aesthetics and Other Essays,* and *Lost Dimensions.*

"... quite a readable fare, in elegant style, informing the reader of what goes on on the mysticism front."

The Journal of Religious Studies

" The book is of interest as a well-articulated expression of what a highly educated Hindu understands by mysticism. The presentation is elegant and the index, containing mostly names, titles and technical words, ample enough."

Vidyajyoti

"... and since Ghose commands a poetically nuanced and most sensitive style, the book has the impact of creative literature, though its approach is descriptive and analytical."

Indian Horizons

ISBN 81-85120-24-2

14 x 22 cms 328 pages Rs. 145